To GOD ALONE be GLORY

Celebrating 200 Years

RPTS Press, Pittsburgh
2008

TABLE of CONTENTS

FOREWORD

The 200th Anniversary Committee of the Reformed Presbyterian Theological Seminary (RPTS), charged with the task of promoting the bicentennial of the seminary that will occur in 2010, agreed that a publication suitable to the occasion needed to be written. Furthermore, the committee agreed that the most appropriate publication would be a *festschrift* honoring the institution rather than an individual. *To God Alone Be Glory* is designed to be a cumulative testimony setting forth reasons to praise the Lord for His sparing the seminary no mercies, and thereby giving the Reformed Presbyterian Church grace upon grace.

There are two types of essays that serve as chapters in the book. The more prominent type might be called personal reflections—the seminary as seen through the eyes of her graduates. Twelve of the seventeen chapters fall into this category. These graduates of RPTS, representing a spread of approximately sixty-five years, reflect on their days in the seminary. Some—Rev. Robert McFarland and Rev. Kenneth Smith—emphasize both continuity and change. Others, such as those written by Rev. Donald Piper and Rev. Walter Swartz, are more anecdotal. The chapters by Rev. Bassam Madany, Rev. Andrew Cooper and Rev. Sung Kug Jung represent God's remarkable use of her graduates, not only through the wider ministry in Christ's Church throughout the world, but also in the variety of denominational backgrounds characteristic of the current student body.

Each contributor was asked to reflect on three questions: First, what were the things you experienced in the seminary that you think contributed to the survival of the seminary in some very dark times? Second, can you describe in terms of your personal experience the attitudes or specific occurrences that you think protected the seminary from the influence of theological liberalism that has destroyed the faithful witness of many American theological seminaries today? Third, based on these two questions, tell the reader about those professors, fellow students, staff and administrators who most influenced you in the shaping of your ministry.

The remaining set of chapters could be defined as topically oriented essays. The committee assigned to six individuals discrete topics that the committee thought needed to be addressed: the relationship of the Synod of the Reformed Presbyterian Church to the Board of Trustees of RPTS, and the expansion of the physical plant (Dr. Robert Copeland); curriculum changes over the years (Dr. Wayne Spear); the development of the seminary library (Librarian Tom Reid); women and the seminary (Mrs. Maryln Black); the wives of seminarians (Mrs. JoAnn Smith); and the wider ministries of the seminary and a vision for the future (President Jerry O'Neill).

As a seminarian of long ago, I too have many memories—some humorous, some inspirational, others regrettable—but today I see the seminary through a double perspective, one that amply supports the theme of God's grace bestowed on the seminary. Today, RPTS shows remarkable progress, building on the faithful ministry of those who served previous generations. Dr. Bruce Stewart completed his tenure as president in 1995 and was succeeded by Dr. Jerry O'Neill, who serves the church today in that capacity. In 1988 RPTS, in cooperation with Geneva College and local urban pastors, played a leading role in the establishment of the

Center for Urban Biblical Ministry (CUBM), a ministry housed at the seminary that provides accredited, undergraduate education for urban students in the city of Pittsburgh. RPTS also provides an off-campus location for Geneva College's Degree Completion Program. In 1998 the seminary initiated its master of theology program.

Recently, the seminary board approved the inception of a doctor of ministry (DMin) degree program. At this time, the first cohort of these students is well on its way to becoming the first DMin graduates of RPTS. The seminary has also achieved a wider and deeper appreciation throughout the Reformed community through its annual international conference on the work of the Westminster Assembly.

When I was a student at RPTS, there were six students in my class and no more than a dozen students all told. All were members of the Reformed Presbyterian Church. During the last decade of the seminary's existence the student body has grown to more than 100 students, representing many denominations and a variety of homelands and ethnic backgrounds.

I thank God for His unswerving faithfulness in preserving this venerable seminary through nearly two centuries. As you read the chapters to follow, I trust that you will come to experience the seminary, her students, faculty and staff, and will offer heartfelt praise to Jesus Christ, the Lord of all life, including the life of the Reformed Presbyterian Theological Seminary, its heritage and its future ministry to the Church and the world.

—Dr. Norman M. Carson

PREFACE

*T*wo hundred years! No small milestone, to be sure. Our forefathers could not have imagined, when they drafted the constitution of the Reformed Presbyterian Theological Seminary in 1807 (classes began in 1810), that 200 years later we would be celebrating two centuries of faithful and fruitful service. Indeed, God has been gracious to us, and it is our great desire to give Him glory for His covenant faithfulness throughout the generations. The title of this book summarizes in five small words the goal of all of us who have contributed to it: *To God Alone Be Glory!*

As we at the seminary put together a 200th Anniversary Committee to plan events surrounding the bicentennial of our beloved seminary, I asked Dr. James Carson to serve as its chairman. No one else is as qualified to serve in such a position. His knowledge and involvement in the life of the seminary and in the church, and the wisdom and leadership gifts that are his, make him the obvious choice. His leadership has been invaluable.

One of the first tasks of the committee was to work on a book that would properly call attention to the work of the seminary, while seeking to give our gracious God the glory due His name. At first this book was envisioned as a historical narrative. However, following the valuable counsel of committee members Dr. Wendell F. and Mrs. Jean W. McBurney, the decision was made to compile a number of short testimonials of God's grace and not proceed with a full-orbed history book.

An early decision made by the committee was that we would seek to provide a book of the highest quality. To do this, two key decisions were made. First, we would solicit the services of Dr. Norman Carson to serve as editor. Dr. Carson, professor emeritus of English at Geneva College, is preeminently qualified to serve in this capacity, and we could not have done what we did without his expertise. In a similar vein, we asked Mrs. Eileen Bechtold from Longmont, Colo., to serve as our graphics designer. I am sure that as you read through the following pages, you will concur with me that her work, also, has been remarkable.

The committee selected individuals who could give firsthand accounts of seminary life over the last seven decades. No attempt has been made in this book to give testimony for years prior to the memories of those now alive who were asked to write. And even as writers have reflected on the last several decades, the goal has not been to provide a comprehensive history, but rather to give personal testimonies of God's amazing grace as evidenced at the seminary over the last half-century.

Writers represent different student eras; different levels of involvement in the life of the seminary—faculty, students, staff, board members and a student wife; and different cultures. But all are united in their deep love for Christ and their deep appreciation for the seminary. As you read the various chapters, you will likely notice certain themes emerge. In large part, these themes are the result of suggestions made by Wendell and Jean McBurney that helped our writers stay on target as they wrote.

Our hope and prayer is that, as you read through this book, your heart will rejoice and your soul will magnify the Lord. *To God Alone Be Glory!*

—Dr. Jerry F. O'Neill

ot unto us, O Lord, not unto us

But to Your name give glory,

Because of Your mercy,

Because of Your truth.

PSALM 115:1

Robert M. Copeland

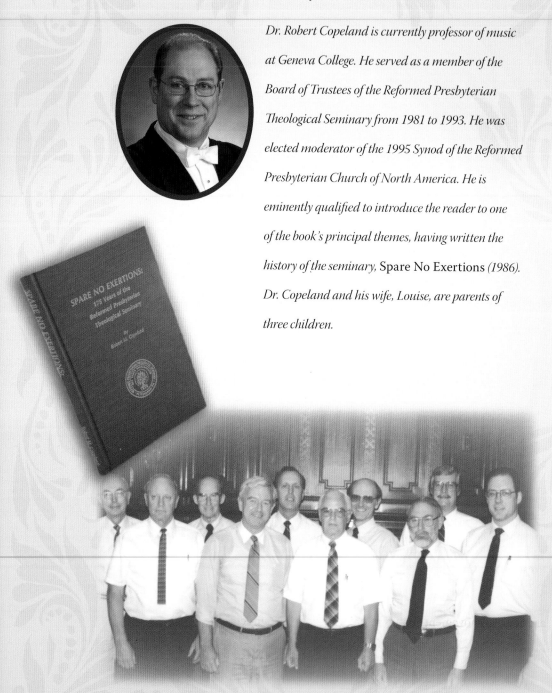

Dr. Robert Copeland is currently professor of music at Geneva College. He served as a member of the Board of Trustees of the Reformed Presbyterian Theological Seminary from 1981 to 1993. He was elected moderator of the 1995 Synod of the Reformed Presbyterian Church of North America. He is eminently qualified to introduce the reader to one of the book's principal themes, having written the history of the seminary, Spare No Exertions (1986). Dr. Copeland and his wife, Louise, are parents of three children.

Two Centuries of Sola Scriptura

My task here is to offer some ruminations from the viewpoint of a historian—neither a pastor nor theologian—about why the Reformed Presbyterian Theological Seminary has remained faithful to the Scriptures and to the Reformed faith when a majority of colleges and seminaries that were established as biblical and Reformed are no longer so. How did this small seminary, serving a tiny denomination, maintain its biblical orthodoxy for two hundred years? In the story of RPTS are found some phenomena that suggest at least a few relevant factors.

Of the reasons one might suggest, the only one of which I am confident is this: God has preserved this institution as a witness for the blessing of the Church of Jesus Christ. No other explanation is totally adequate.

In acting in the affairs of men and women, however, God normally uses people and events as secondary causes, acting through both their wise and their foolish actions and decisions to accomplish His will. Let me suggest four ways that secondary causes have contributed to the theological stability of RPTS.

First, *Invisibility*. Because of the size of the seminary and the Reformed Presbyterian Church, the seminary has always "flown beneath the radar" in American educational and theological affairs. We were small enough that the leaders of great movements could remain unaware of our activities and our theology. Even today, the large seminaries of the major denominations attract the attention of the media; their controversies are magnified, their policies scrutinized, their decisions praised or blamed by unbelievers according to current fashion. For example, in recent decades Concordia Seminary (Lutheran) in St. Louis and all of the Southern Baptist seminaries have been pressed by the media and the public to adopt more liberal positions and suppress conservative theology. Orthodoxy has been mocked and orthodox faculty and trustees excoriated. The Reformed Presbyterian Theological Seminary has simply been too small for notice. While we have been blessed with knowledgeable, wise, respected and godly faculty, on the whole we have not had faculty who were famous in the eyes of the world, none whose reputations could lift them up in pride or arouse the envy of their colleagues. Without question, being small has its advantages.

Second, *Purpose.* The purpose of RPTS for two centuries has been to prepare pastors rather than theologians. To be sure, the seminary has always insisted on scholarship, as the denomination has insisted on an educated ministry. Students study biblical languages, systematic and biblical theology, and related disciplines, but RPTS has never forgotten that the purpose of these disciplines in a seminary, in contrast to a university, is to produce men who can preach soundly and can shepherd souls. Some other seminaries have forgotten that purpose and aim to produce scholarly experts who will write learned tomes that win the admiration of other experts. Scholarship, need it be said, is a calling of God and makes use of His good gifts; the Church has often been edified and strengthened through the work of scholars.

> *RPTS has never forgotten that the purpose of these disciplines in a seminary…is to produce men who can preach soundly and can shepherd souls.*

Some of the most foolish and most dangerous books by scholars, however, are those written to impress other experts. A theological seminary must be rooted in the *practice* of Christian theology if it is to remain true to the *spirit and goal* of Christian theology.

Third, *Control.* The Synod of the Reformed Presbyterian Church has always exercised a firm but not oppressive hand guiding the seminary. Much of this guidance has come through a board elected by the Synod, and this board has always been actively involved in all aspects of the seminary. The original Constitution of 1807 provided for the election by Synod of three "superintendents" to oversee virtually every aspect of seminary operations. There was, after all, no administrator and only one professor to teach the entire curriculum. By 1845, this board was reorganized and called the Board of Inspectors. Part of their responsibility was to conduct the end-of-year examinations that helped to ensure orthodoxy on the part of the faculty as well as the students. In the 1820s, at least, these examinations lasted from a week to ten days, but by the 1890s only three days. When the seminary was revived in 1856 after a brief hiatus, a Board of Superintendents was elected. Their responsibility in the examinations was reduced to that of observers

as the faculty conducted the oral examinations. From 1882 to 1888, every member of the board also graded all of the written examinations, a reform soon abandoned for practical reasons. Until well into the twentieth century, the board selected or approved the textbooks for most of the subjects. As the seminary matured and the faculty increased, and as the social and legal status of theological institutions changed, the responsibilities of the board evolved from being essentially a standing committee of Synod to being fiduciaries for a legal entity—in a word, Trustees. Not until 1976, however, was the title changed.

Regardless of title, the board, Janus-like, has functioned in two directions: toward the seminary, conveying the directives, policies and advice of the Synod; and toward the Synod, apprising the church of the needs and progress of the seminary and serving as the advocate for the faculty and students in the courts of the church. The movements toward new or remodeled facilities have been led by the Trustees—for example, the sale of the Memorial Building on the North Side in 1922 and the purchase of the Durbin Horne estate in 1924; the remodeling and renovation of the building in 1960-65; the construction of the library in the 1970s. Fundraising efforts, whether for routine expenses in the long years before 1919 (the creation of "Synod's Budget") or for capital campaigns, have been spearheaded by the Trustees. A committee of the board worked closely with the faculty to redesign the curriculum in the early 1950s, as they had in the past as well. The board, in short, has been sensitive to the welfare of the students and faculty and to the needs of the instructional program. Within the tight circle of friends and extended family in the Synod and the denomination, any move toward heterodoxy could be identified and eliminated expeditiously.

Synod's guidance of the seminary has also been more direct. A key factor in the faithfulness of the seminary has been that the entire Synod elects every full-time professor from among its own ranks. This ensures that the faculty have the confidence of the Synod with respect to orthodoxy as well as gifts; a "stealth candidate" is nearly impossible in the small circle of the Synod. The fact that all faculty are elected for renewable terms—three years initially and seven years thereafter—ensures that they *continue* to enjoy the confidence of the Synod. Virtually all of the professors have had extensive pastoral experience. The majority of institutional funding has historically come from the denomination as well, with no large endowments or gifts from wealthy industrialists, to tempt the seminary to back away from denominational positions on issues.

Denominations that have kept only a loose rein (or none at all) on their seminaries have left them open to theological drift and partisan take-overs. Seminaries that

Synod's guidance of the seminary....

have been founded as independent, nondenominational, or interdenominational have too often drifted out of the current of orthodoxy. Those that have sought famous theologians or philosophers for their faculty have found that philosophy and academic theology do not substitute for faithful orthodoxy.

But being guarded and guided by a denomination is no guarantee of theological faithfulness if the denomination slips out of the current. Methodist, Presbyterian, and Episcopal seminaries that have had close ties to their denominations have lost their theological integrity, roughly simultaneously with that same loss in their denominations. In some cases, the seminaries have been the catalysts for drift as their graduates have imbibed the spirit of faculty "liberalism" and led their churches astray. In other cases, the seminaries have followed the lead of their denominations in decline and defection. Princeton Theological Seminary was the most prominent bastion of orthodox Calvinism through most of the nineteenth century, but when the Presbyterian General Assembly embraced "toleration" rather than biblical orthodoxy, the seminary was reorganized (1929) to dilute Reformed doctrine and make it only one voice among many. If RPTS has remained faithful, it has been possible only because the denomination has remained faithful.

Some defections have come about through denominational mergers rather than carelessness. For example, Service Seminary was founded in 1794 in rural Beaver County, Pennsylvania, to serve the Associate Presbyterian Church. It was moved successively to Canonsburg, Pennsylvania; Xenia, Ohio; and St. Louis, Missouri. When the Associate Presbyterian Church merged with the Associate

Reformed Presbyterian Church to form the United Presbyterian Church in 1858, their seminary was merged as well, creating the Xenia Theological Seminary (later Pittsburgh-Xenia), which was still reasonably orthodox. When the United Presbyterian Church merged with the Presbyterian Church in the USA in 1958, Pittsburgh-Xenia was merged with Western Theological Seminary to form the present, and far more liberal, Pittsburgh Theological Seminary.

Fourth, *Scottish stubbornness.* The Reformed Presbyterian Church was forged in the struggles for political and religious freedom in Scotland in the sixteenth and seventeenth centuries. The bitter controversies of the Thirty Years' War in Germany and the Wars of Religion in France were matched by the bloody persecution of Covenanters in the Killing Times (1660-88) in Scotland. When the nation finally threw off the yoke of Stuart oppression in 1688, a significant majority of the nation turned away from the religious controversies altogether and adopted a "broad" approach in the national church. Only a minority maintained their original principles, and this minority became the Reformed Presbytery. During the previous decades, some 18,000 of them had suffered torture, death, imprisonment and banishment for religious and political liberty, and when the Revolution came, they refused to yield religious liberty to Parliament just as they had refused to yield it up to the king. The majority of Scots were soon swept up in the Scottish Enlightenment, which dominated education, society and economics for generations and influenced the Church of Scotland away from the gospel and toward the goddess Reason. While Reformed Presbyterians were not impervious to the seductions of the Enlightenment, they were relatively unaffected, because only members of the established church were allowed to attend the universities. Reformed Presbyterian ministers were trained largely in the Netherlands.

When brought to America, either as immigrants or transported as prisoners, they maintained their familiar mindset, which included a focus on biblical truth and an insistence that although human learning is valuable, it is always subject to correction by Scripture and not by the state or by fashion. This has remained a hallmark of Reformed Presbyterian thinking for three and a half centuries, and it has been implemented in its theological education. It still is.

Thus, the fidelity of the Reformed Presbyterian Theological Seminary to biblical and Reformed doctrine through two centuries does not reflect an ignorance of or a disdain for new theories, information and philosophies. It reflects a stubborn determination to hang on to what is valuable about the old and not to be seduced by the new and untried. It reflects sponsorship by a small denomination determined to maintain "the faith once delivered to the saints." It reflects a close sense of Christian community marked by mutual accountability. It has remained faithful to the scriptural proverb: "Remove not the ancient landmark which thy fathers have set up."

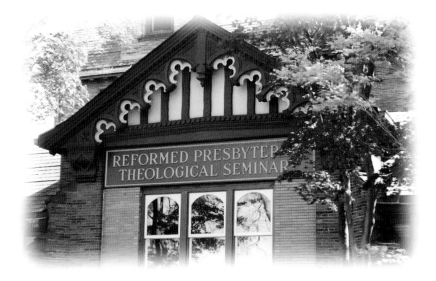

Paul E. Faris

A Kansas farm boy, Paul Faris graduated from RPTS in 1945. He served the RP Church in three pastorates: Quinter and Sterling, Kansas, and Lisbon, New York. He was moderator of the RP Synod in 1983 and 1984. Here we catch a glimpse of the "old guard" at RPTS. Pastor Faris writes movingly about his love for pastoral care gained at the seminary. He also emphasizes the need for "balance" in the denomination, a conviction born out of his seminary experience. Paul Faris is the father of three children.

CHAPTER 2

The Blessing of Balance

The story of the Reformed Presbyterian Theological Seminary (RPTS) is not the dream or shadow of one man. Instead, it is the vision of a portion of God's people who came out of the persecution years in the land of Scotland where earthly kings tried to usurp the place of Christ as the Rock and Head of His Church—the King of kings and Lord of all of life! The Covenanters' struggle for Christ's Crown and Covenant was fresh in the minds of men of our American denomination as they realized how this new land was overlooking that cardinal truth of Christ's Kingship over the nation. They saw that the absence of this belief would lead again to restrictions in the freedom to think, live and worship according to the vision God gave our forefathers.

That passionate vision motivated our denomination to establish a seminary in order that we might have an educated ministry, equipping pastors who could articulate and promote the distinctives of our denomination. In its history, the locations and professors have changed several times to meet the needs.

During my student days in the 1940s, the seminary was well settled in the Durbin Horne mansion that the church purchased in 1924. Dr. R.J.G. McKnight, appointed in 1916 as a professor of Greek and Hebrew and then in 1928 as president, was the "resident" professor. The Synod in 1929 appointed four men, W.J. Coleman, John Coleman, Robert Park, and J. Boyd Tweed to serve as professors with President McKnight. That very year marked the end of a decade-long seminary war at Princeton Seminary with liberalism the victor. My professors were well aware of such dangers. President McKnight, in his studies in Germany for his doctorate, directly encountered the revival of liberalism in our day.

That faculty team-taught together at RPTS during the theological debates of the 1930s, the economic depression and World War II. Those professors appointed in 1929, with the exception of Boyd Tweed, were my instructors. Two of the professors were also serving as professors at Geneva College; Dr. John Coleman and Dr. Robert Park commuted one day weekly to teach at RPTS. Dr. W.J. Coleman, living on Pittsburgh's North Side and still active in his 90s, gave a day each week to teach the seminarians.

I was allowed by my Kansas draft board to begin seminary in the fall of 1942 because my board believed that if the war continued, they would need replacements in the chaplaincy program. Many other draft boards did not grant that exemption to potential seminarians but instead drafted them to active duty. I was the only first-year student starting that fall. Perhaps it was the shortage of funds, but the

seminary did not provide a cook that year. We students discovered that we would have responsibilities for meal preparation and operation of the heating system; those experiences could provide additional stories. My years at RPTS, 1942–45, may not have been its golden years, but in God's planning they revealed to me what ministry should be developed with the life He had given me.

Committed to training men equipped to promote our distinctives, the professors in our class emphasized those distinctives, particularly the Kingship of Christ over the nation. W.J. Coleman had spent years traveling and lecturing, proclaiming, "If we don't change the U.S. Constitution, we will again experience what our forefathers suffered in Scotland." The other professors also gave years to serving on the denomination's Witness Committee and lecturing and writing on the Kingship of Christ over the nation. One professor recommended that, as preachers, we use the fifth Sabbath in a month to preach on one of the distinctives, and thereby cover the distinctives each year in our preaching. I actually did that in my first years as a pastor.

In his course on the meditation of Psalms in worship, Dr. R.J.G. McKnight stressed the explanation of the Psalms in the worship services; he emphasized that, to sing the Psalms, we needed to understand them. W.J. Coleman encouraged us to cultivate musical training in the families to enhance our worship of God with the *a cappella* singing of the Psalms. He reasoned that, while other churches spend money for organs, we should spend money on music lessons so that our children could read music and sing in the worship of God.

At the end of my first semester in my final year, W.J. Coleman died after a short illness. Dr. Delber H. Elliott, pastor at the Central Pittsburgh RPC, was appointed to fill out that year as professor of pastoral theology; later, his time as professor was extended to 1950. Dr. Coleman, professor of pastoral theology, had completed our study of R.J. George's three  volumes, *Lectures in Pastoral Theology*; the third book, entitled *The Covenanter Vision*, especially emphasized the Covenanter distinctives. With that study complete, Dr. Elliott decided to draw on his pastoral experiences for class lectures. During Dr. Elliott's pastorate in Winchester, Kansas, many young people entered pastoral and mission service; the Synod then appointed him as secretary of the Forward Movement, through which he encouraged the church's evangelistic and mission efforts for seven years. When the Central Pittsburgh congregation called him, he resumed the pastoral ministry. Through Dr. Elliott's lectures on the pastoral ministry, God touched my life and cultivated the pastoral gifts He had planted in me for my service.

Another influential experience during my first year at seminary was my being very ill with pneumonia and sulfa fever. My professors were quite supportive during that illness. Experiencing the receiving side of bedfast hospital care provided for me a needed perspective for the pastoral ministry to the sick. That circumstance coupled with Dr. Elliott's emphasis on pastoral care shaped my ministry. Later when he was a guest minister during a communion season in my first pastorate, Dr. Elliott continued to give me that encouraging pastoral focus.

The greatest satisfaction I experienced in the pastorate was calling on individuals and families, in their homes or other places, and learning to know them and their needs in their daily experiences, especially times of trials, death or tragedy. As I knew the people and sensed the needs, I could draw on the Scriptures to encourage, comfort or even convict them, as God seemed to be dealing with them and as God used me with appropriate responses and prayer.

During the time that I was writing this chapter, I experienced another near-death illness and hospitalization; through it, I have realized anew God's purposes; now I labor in therapy to regain enough strength to serve Him with the talents I came to realize initially through the men God placed in my life at RPTS. Yes, even from the hospital bed I can encourage and minister to the medical team ministering to me.

My current therapy routine, teaching me anew the importance of balance, has stimulated my meditation on balance in the church. Our testimony states, "No church is perfect." Neither is any seminary.

As I view our current society, I am reminded of my professor's warning that if we did not straighten out the U.S. Constitution and did not acknowledge Christ's Kingship, we would see the consequences and experience what our forefathers suffered in Scotland. On the horizon, I think we are seeing it. This is not a dead issue for the church. Our culture is not Christian, and our government is polytheistic. For example, with the hate crimes legislation, we may well face persecution that could affect Christians in any walk of life.

During my training years, when the emphasis was on proclaiming the Kingship of Christ to the nation, our denomination was losing its covenant children and congregations were dying. Balance was needed; we needed not only to proclaim the Kingship of Christ at the national level but also to proclaim the gospel to individuals, families and local congregations. We needed to have that strong foundation to support strong, faithful individuals, families and congregations who could impact the national scene. We needed to build from the bottom up.

Our denomination and seminary have continued simply because of the grace of God and the work of the Spirit of God in balancing the church. I have called my time at the seminary the "changing of the guard." I feel that during that era there began steps to balance the strong emphasis on the church's distinctives with other truths and needs. I have observed over the decades God's providence working toward that balance in the church and in the seminary's mission and emphasis.

My own service in the church at large, based on Synod's assignments, was on the evangelism committee and the publication board. Our evangelism committee worked with Remo Robb, who served as Synod's Home Mission Secretary and also Young People's Secretary. During the late forties and fifties, Remo Robb, through the Covenanter Crusade, challenged us to double the membership by encouraging each member to draw in another member. We had a problem, however, in accomplishing that because we were continuing to lose members; we needed a solution to that problem. I did not have training in the seminary for that solution.

The Navigators influenced Ken Smith, a young Pittsburgh pastor, and some of our seminary students when Dawson Trotman worked in the follow-up labor of Billy Graham's Crusade in Pittsburgh. Young pastors such as Don McClurkin and Paul Robb, who were influenced while in Pittsburgh, brought their enthusiasm to their service on the evangelism committee. The Navigator influence spread and influenced many of us in our daily walk with God, the topical memory system, and evangelism and follow-up work.

The denomination also upgraded its Christian education ministry, seeking to train children and members and to develop curricula. I think that the denomination's

growing emphasis in evangelism, home missions, and Christian education helped to balance the church.

These efforts affected not only the denomination but also the seminary. The seminary broadened its program to prepare short-term mission workers, some of whom went to Cyprus in the late sixties. In more recent decades, the seminary has emphasized training men in the Reformed faith and in biblical theology. Perhaps partly to help its financial base, the seminary broadened its task to train men outside the RPCNA. The seminary's pursuit of academic accreditation brought an emphasis on its academic standards. All of these movements within the denomination and the seminary have been part of that "balancing" work to equip men for the ministry and to provide an institution that supports the health of the denomination. Just as physical therapy can be painful, so the church has known the pain of the labor necessary to get and maintain our balance.

As I consider memories, particularly of my seminary training, I believe it was truly a special time in the history and life of this institution. It is not boasting in man but in the sovereign grace of God that allows us to celebrate 200 years of service that the Reformed Presbyterian Theological Seminary has rendered.

Bassam M. Madany

Five years after Paul Faris's studies at RPTS, Rev. Bassam M. Madany arrived, the first to come from a Reformed Presbyterian mission, although not the first student from overseas. His view of the seminary, therefore, was unique. Not only was he able to master the English language, but also he achieved a solid foundation in the Reformed faith.

After serving briefly in the Reformed Presbyterian Church, Bassam became the Arabic minister of the Back-to-God Hour (1958–94). Together with his wife he continues his ministry through Middle East Resources. God has blessed Bassam Madany and his wife, Shirley, with six children.

Bassam & Shirley W. Madany

An Introduction to Islam

CHAPTER 3

From Syria to Pittsburgh

September 1, 1950, will always be a memorable day in my life. I arrived in the USA after spending three weeks on an American Export Line ship that had left Beirut on August 8, with stops in Alexandria, Naples, Genoa, Marseilles, Boston, and New York. Two weeks later, after visiting my relatives in Bridgeport, Connecticut, I left by train for Pittsburgh, arriving late on the night of September 17.

From my first moment at the Reformed Presbyterian Theological Seminary, I felt welcomed. The rest of the student body had arrived some time before and were already settled in their rooms. I was shown to my place, which was in a rather large bedroom that housed several other seminarians. Fellow student Norman Carson drove me the next day to downtown Pittsburgh, where I made my first purchases of theological textbooks at the United Presbyterian Bookstore.

The atmosphere at 7418 Penn Avenue was very friendly. My fellow students were eager to offer advice regarding academic or other topics. Having lived all my early years in Syria and Lebanon, almost everything now seemed new to me. American meals were quite different from the Levantine cuisine to which I was accustomed. Also, the English I knew and spoke was mostly of British origin, so now I had to learn American pronunciation and spelling.

I am very grateful to the Lord for having guided me to the Reformed Presbyterian Theological Seminary. When I felt called to the ministry in 1948, I applied to study at the Near East School of Theology in Beirut, Lebanon. Thanks to advice from the Rev. Tom Semple, a missionary from Northern Ireland who was teaching at the mission schools in Latakia, I did not pursue steps to enroll at that school. Rather, I began the process of enrolling at RPTS. Thanks also to the help of Kenneth and Marjorie Sanderson and Eunice McClurkin, who were teaching at the Mission Schools in Latakia, and my uncle Henry of Bridgeport, who provided the Affidavit of Support, I obtained the student visa to come to America. My theological training at the seminary proved to be of invaluable help in my lifelong radio ministry to the Arabic-speaking world.

At first, it was not easy to be in the same class listening to lectures with seniors, middlers and juniors. During the first semester in 1950, the combined class was dealing with the last part of Systematic Theology (the doctrines of the church and the Last Things)! What made it even more difficult was that all my previous studies had been in French and Arabic. I had taken English but only as a third language, which simply included grammar and literature. Now I had to listen to lectures that were predominantly theological, sprinkled with Hebrew, Greek and Latin expressions. By the end of the first academic year, however, I was quite at home in theological English.

All the members of the faculty were committed to the supreme and final authority of the Word of God. The basics in a theological curriculum were given by these men who had faithfully served the Lord for many years. They would share with us anecdotes about some of the theological struggles that were going on within Protestant denominations. I shall never forget the pathos in the words of Dr. McKnight while speaking about the last days of Dr. Machen. This great defender of the faith had sent a post-card to Dr. McKnight from his hospital in South Dakota ending with, "Saved by grace."

Around two decades had passed since the reor-ganization of Princeton Seminary, but that tragic event was still fresh in the mind of Dr. J.B. Willson. He would recount the plight of the widow of Robert Dick Wilson of Princeton Seminary. She was in a difficult financial situa-tion, as her late husband had lost all rights to his pension

My theological training at the seminary proved to be of invaluable help in my lifelong radio ministry to the Arabic-speaking world.

upon leaving that institution. When Dr. Willson heard about my special interest in learning more about the errors of Dispensationalism, he arranged for me to meet with Dr. Oswald Allis, one of the founders of Westminster Seminary. Having gone several times to preach in RP congregations in Philadelphia, I used one of those opportunities to visit with Professor Allis. He was a model for the depth of his learning and his total commitment to the historic Christian faith. I treasure his book, *Prophecy and the Church*, which details the errors of the Dispensational hermeneutics. Studying this book encouraged me to audit a semester course on Dispensationalism taught by Dr. John Gerstner of Pittsburgh-Xenia Seminary, who dealt with the subject from a historical-theological perspective.

I remember Dr. McKnight's comments on my first student sermon that I had delivered the night before at the Connellsville Reformed Presbyterian Church. It was not easy for me to preach in English for the first time in my life! Dr. McKnight

remarked that I had done well in my delivery and exhibited an evangelistic spirit throughout my message.

In my junior year Dr. Park suggested that we write a major paper on a subject in Church history. I chose the correspondence of John Calvin. I learned that the Carnegie Library in Pittsburgh had several volumes of Calvin's letters in French, published during the nineteenth century. I borrowed those tomes and, working on the project, I discovered that the Genevan Reformer was much more than a theologian; he was a pastor with a warm heart. I was extremely touched by his comforting words to the mother of several sons who were imprisoned in France on account of their loyalty to the Reformed faith.

The study of systematic theology had a special place at the RP Seminary. I am very thankful to have sat at the feet of Dr. Roy Fullerton. While he was not an original thinker, he did an excellent job in imparting to us a keen sense of seeing the interrelationship of the various doctrines of the Christian faith. He led us through the three volumes of Charles Hodge and Louis Berkhof's one volume in this discipline. And with further readings of major theological works, Dr. Fullerton left us well prepared to meet the challenges of the fifties and the sixties. He showed his wisdom in making us study Cornelius Van Til's *The New Modernism*. Thus, we realized that, great as their reputation was, neither Emil Bruner nor Karl Barth was leading the church in the right direction through their neo-orthodoxy. The history of the rest of the century would vindicate Van Til's thesis.

It would be hard for me to say who influenced me the most during my three-year stay in Pittsburgh. I would credit the entire faculty and the student body for the strong impression they made upon me in their devotion to Protestant, and specifically Reformed, orthodoxy. Furthermore, their loyalty to the Covenanter heritage was very clear.

As we approach the 200th anniversary of the founding of the Reformed Presbyterian Theological Seminary, it is worth asking what has kept it loyal to orthodox Protestantism. Ultimately, it is by God's grace and wonderful providential guidance that He enabled the seminary to cling to "the faith that was once for all entrusted to the saints" (Jude 3b). But human factors must not be discounted. I would like to suggest two:

1. A close link between the Reformed Presbyterian Church and the seminary. The seminary has always been very dear to the hearts and minds of the membership of the Reformed Presbyterian Church. I experienced that in my travels to many parts of the country, and in Winnipeg, Canada, where I spent two summers working at the

loyalty to the Covenanter heritage

Covenanter Church in that metropolis. Not only Synod, but the whole church remained vitally interested in the life of its seminary. That was quite tangible even in small things, as when we received food gifts every fall from the nearby constituency.

2. An awareness of current theological trends. The Reformed Presbyterian Church and its theological seminary were quite aware of the tremendous theological upheavals that were taking place within the mainline Protestant denominations. The decades of the 1920s, 1930s and 1940s witnessed the triumph of Modernism in the Presbyterian Church USA. The Covenanters were adequately forewarned about the disastrous consequences of relinquishing the fundamentals of the Christian faith. If they were to preserve what had been handed down to them across the centuries, they were to cling to the authority of the Bible and maintain their confessional heritage by adhering to the Westminster Standards, as well as their own particular testimony. The seminary has remained faithful across these two hundred years. The church and the seminary will continue to receive the Lord's blessings as long as they keep faithful to the affirmations of the Protestant Reformation: *Sola Scriptura, Solus Christus, Sola Fide, Sola Gratia, and Soli Deo Gloria.*

Kenneth G. Smith

Kenneth G. Smith's days at RPTS preceded a time of transition there. Here he foresees this change. Following graduation he became the pastor of the Central Pittsburgh congregation (1952–57). For the next fifteen years he served the denomination in a variety of offices, including those of education and evangelism, and on many boards and committees. He ministered in Cyprus from 1972 to 1974. In 1982 he was elected moderator of the Synod. Since 1974 he has pastored two congregations: Covenant Fellowship, Pittsburgh (1975–92) and Syracuse, New York (1993–2002). Dr. Smith and his wife, Floy, are parents of three children.

CHAPTER 4

From the Old Building to the New: An Analogy

When I entered the Reformed Presbyterian Theological Seminary in the fall of 1949, I was under the sense of the call of Jesus Christ to become a minister of the gospel. Because I was a lifetime member of the Reformed Presbyterian Church of North America, it did not occur to me to enroll in any other seminary, and I was taken under care by my presbytery as a student of theology.

As an old denomination with a rich legacy both in doctrine and defense of the faith, the Reformed Presbyterian Church carefully guarded its testimony to the rule of Jesus Christ over all of life, including civil government. I was committed to this legacy, and I looked forward to what I would learn in our seminary.

One encouragement to me centered on my fellow students, most of whom I had known for many years. Norman Carson and I first met in 1938 at Winona Lake, Indiana, at a denominational conference. I roomed with Roy Blackwood and Jim Carson during college days. Harold Harrington, Tom Wilson, Joe Caskey, and I had been classmates at Geneva College. So there was deep comradeship among us, and today I continue to treasure it. Upperclassmen included friends such as Willard McMillan and Joe Hill, both of whom would strongly influence my life and ministry. I could name others who followed, and the positive influence was the same. We kept the ping-pong table busy after lunch, and volleyball was in when the weather suited.

But it is the relationship that the seminary sustains with our denomination that looms supremely important in keeping the institution true to the historical Christian faith. To say that the denomination at that time was ingrown would not be an exaggeration. As descendants of the Covenanters and Killing Times of Scotland in the 1600s, we had deep roots; but persecution can result in a defensive posture. The denomination had been numerically declining since the 1890s, and a "hold-the-line" mentality had unwittingly overtaken us. Some cried out for renewal and positive witness; and at that time the denomination was involved in seeking a Christian amendment to the secular Constitution of the United States,

> ⟨❧⟩
>
> *The relationship that the seminary sustains with our denomination looms supremely important in keeping the institution true to the historical Christian faith.*
>
> ⟨❧⟩

regularly lobbying members of Congress to present such a bill to the Congress. This preoccupation with our own concerns, however, kept us to a large extent turned inward rather than outward. As seminary students, many of whom were veterans of World War II, we wrestled with our own purpose in going into the ministry. What was the outlook?

Now this ingrownness was both a bane and a boon. While we clearly needed a fresh outpouring of the Holy Spirit to refresh us and clarify our vision, we also escaped many of the issues battering the traditional seminaries of our land. Fundamentally those issues had their roots in the higher criticism of Scripture, questioning the historicity of much of the Bible, and also the new influence of Darwinism. Both movements came in the mid- to late-1800s and had, and still have, devastating effects on the American church. I suggest two reasons why we were protected from these things. First, we continued

to be totally committed to the inerrancy of Scripture, but our attention was largely occupied by internal issues. Our battles, therefore, differed from those being waged within our sister evangelical denominations, and it was these issues that kept us occupied.

Second, we were protected by our commitment to biblical worship, meaning in our case an unquestioned allegiance to the singing of the Psalms of the Bible. History seems to show that many, if not most, heresies came into the church through the lyrics of their hymns. The Reformed Presbyterian Church cannot boast at this point, but it never wavered from its confession that the Psalms of the Bible preserve, as well as encourage, the Church. The seminary, being closely tied to the Reformed Presbyterian Church (all professors were and are chosen by its Synod, not by an independent board), taught us the significance and value of these Songs of the Kingdom.

As indicated above, it was a difficult time for the denomination and its institutions. Many of its youth had bolted during the 1930s and '40s. But following World War II seminaries in general were full, and ours boasted a larger enrollment than it had in many years. Occasionally I would hear reference to that fact made on the floor of the Synod as indicating clear evidence of renewal being on the way. There was, however, much that needed to be "reformed." The seminary was no exception. Let me describe it by means of an analogy.

In 1924 the denomination purchased a large mansion in the East End of Pittsburgh which had at one time belonged to Durbin Horne, a member of the Joseph Horne family who founded the most prestigious department store in downtown Pittsburgh. And a marvelous building it was—beautiful in design, solid in construction, lavishly appointed, and set within the context of lovely landscaping. It stood as a picture of wealth and prosperity of a now bygone Pittsburgh.

By mid-century, however, time had taken its toll. President McKnight did his best to keep the aged boiler functioning so we could keep warm, but we often had to rely on one of the gas log fireplaces that had become eroded, emitting fumes that produced drowsiness. The electrical system boasted classical chandeliers, but not the kind that helped one find books in the uncataloged library. Once the plumbing had been the best, but that time was long past. Neither the dumbwaiter nor the elevator functioned consistently. So here was a wonderful building with a rich heritage, reflective of a wonderful past, and yet in desperate need of refurbishment.

In many ways our seminary echoed the health of our denomination: a wonderfully rich heritage, but desperately in need of renewal. Her institutions, including the seminary and its building and program, shared the need.

In spite of the decline in the seminary, I am grateful to the Lord for not having led some of us to another seminary, though at times we explored that possibility. These were "our times," and while scholarship did not always excel and while much of the praxis required of a reputable professional rather than graduate institution was absent, yet there was much to commend it. Dr. McKnight's lectures held our interest, and his concern that we learn the Psalms was buttressed by his regular exposition of them. From time to time we had guest lecturers, such as Dr. Withrow of Ohio State University, Professor John Gerstner of Pittsburgh-Xenia Seminary, and Dr. Cornelius Van Til of Westminster Seminary. I believe that Dr. Oswald Allis also helped us by his lecture on biblical hermeneutics. All of these scholars to whom we were introduced at RPTS gave us reasons to believe in and embrace the historical Christian faith as given to us in Scripture and as handed down to us from our rich denominational heritage.

In God's providence, He sent renewal, and today the seminary building still exhibits its rich past, having had the derelict features such as lighting, heating, plumbing and elevator replaced. Extensive remodeling of the interior has preserved the beauty of the building while enhancing its function as a seminary. And this says nothing of the spacious addition to the library. So the analogy still rings true. Like the building, the educational program maintains its historical and theological legacy while addressing the challenges of the twenty-first century with qualified and dedicated faculty and staff. Today the Reformed Presbyterian Theological Seminary exists as a vibrant institution, true to its biblical legacy, relevant to a waiting world, and challenging to an eager student body. I thank Jesus Christ for sending His renewal!

...relevant to a waiting world

Robert H. McFarland

*By 1955, when Robert McFarland entered RPTS,
the changes predicted by Kenneth Smith had begun
to appear. Pastor McFarland recounts the changes
happening during his student days and emphasizes
the theological continuity that exists between him and
his forebears, a continuity also seen in the seminary.
In addition to his pastorates in the Rose Point,
Pennsylvania, and Quinter and Topeka, Kansas,
congregations, he served as director of Educational
Services and Youth Ministries (1983–87) and on many
boards and committees of the Synod. He served as
moderator of Synod in 2003. Robert McFarland and
his wife, Georgia, are parents of three children.*

CHAPTER 5

The Turtle on the Fencepost

My father, a Covenanter pastor, once told me that his father, who completed his formal schooling at the third grade, was his first "seminary of theological truth." My grandfather had to discontinue his formal education to help his mother manage their farm; still, when he had his own family he instructed his six sons and three daughters in the Scriptures, Psalm memorization, the *Westminster Confession of Faith*, and the *Catechism*. My father found it such a blessing to attend the Reformed Presbyterian Theological Seminary because its president, Dr. R.J.G. McKnight, with his knowledge of the original languages and his scholarship, always reaffirmed my minimally educated grandfather's theological training. Because my father had already received this biblical training at home in Oklahoma as a young boy from his father, the continuity between generations became clear.

As the Reformed Presbyterian Theological Seminary comes to this bicentennial celebration of its founding, it is appropriate to consider the reasons that the foundations of the seminary remain sound after two centuries of existence.

How did my grandfather's instruction match so well that of the seminary? It is no accident. If one sees a turtle sitting on the top of a six-foot post, he must conclude that somebody put him there. In the case of this seminary, it has been the Reformed Presbyterian Church that has put the turtle on the post. The denomination has carefully maintained the examination of the professors who have had the key role in continuing the Reformed Presbyterian Theological Seminary as a pillar of truth for 200 years. To understand the foundational continuity of the seminary one must understand the character of the Reformed Presbyterian (Covenanter) Church, which is a confessional church. Its ordained officers believe in and accept the *Westminster Confession of Faith* and the denomination's *Testimony.* The church requires of its members clear adherence to the Word of God as being inerrant and inspired.

Seminaries are often tempted to reject the authority structure placed over them and to introduce in their teaching some practice or teaching that has not yet been approved by the denominational courts, ceasing to teach these matters only when a higher court confronts or sues them. As seminary board members and faculty serve the denomination that is supporting and controlling them, they may observe unrest in the denomination on established theological positions and may feel pressure to begin teaching a position not yet approved by a court of the church.

I was scarcely aware of such pressures when I entered the seminary. When I arrived at the Reformed Presbyterian Theological Seminary I had already been asked by my session to acknowledge my adherence to the doctrines of the faith and the subordinate doctrines of the church. Thus, I joined the others in the student body who were seeking ways to proclaim more clearly what we believed, praying for clarity in presenting the testimony of the denomination. The professors themselves had already embraced and publicly professed adherence to these

I joined the others in the student body who were seeking ways to proclaim more clearly what we believed, praying for clarity in presenting the testimony.

doctrines upon becoming communicant members of the Reformed Presbyterian Church. As their students we were coming to learn how to communicate and defend the particular doctrines.

But RPTS is not immune from doctrinal disputes. Dr. Robert Copeland wrote in his book *Spare No Exertions* that in one instance two seminary professors had such intense disagreement over the biblical teaching on the role of deacons that Synod had to intervene in the conflict. The point to be emphasized is that Synod did intervene, thus asserting its rightful position in overseeing the seminary curriculum.

In the mid-1980s, the Synod of the Reformed Presbyterian Church successfully met one challenge to become less Reformed Presbyterian when they received the request of the seminary board to appoint some who were not members of the Reformed Presbyterian Church to the Board of Trustees. Those proposing this to the Synod felt this was the right way to broaden the base of support and gain additional students and more visibility. It was the Synod exercising its control of the seminary that determined the course of action. In 1984, after much discussion, the Synod agreed to add three who were not members of the Reformed Presbyterian denomination to the Board of Trustees of the seminary. But a special resolution

brought the matter back to the floor of the Synod in 1985, where the board membership was again limited to men who are elders in the Reformed Presbyterian Church. A President's Council that includes those in the broader Reformed and evangelical community was then established.

Requiring all seminary trustees to be members of the sponsoring denomination provides a biblical court to which all in the seminary must submit. Having this direct oversight is a major reason why the seminary is what it is today.

Nothing can replace the importance that the Reformed Presbyterian Theological Seminary has placed on seeking professors who have had pastoral experience in local congregations. In the midst of trends in other denominations to send scholars who have not served as pastors into the professorship, the Reformed Presbyterian Church and its seminary have seen the value of pastors teaching pastors.

One of our seminary presidents, in a lecture to the students, cautioned them of the danger of becoming scholars, but not pastoring the people in their congregation. He cautioned our pastors who have learned Hebrew and Greek not to use it as a demonstration of personal brilliance by doing "Hebrew Push-Ups" behind the pulpit—a show of scholarship without clarity or content.

One does not have to look far in Reformed circles to find denominations that have discontinued denominationally controlled seminaries and colleges. Because of this trend, there are seminaries that elect their own Board of Trustees. They believe that they can avoid repetition of the decline of formerly biblical seminaries such as Princeton and other seminaries under denominational control.

value of pastors teaching pastors

The great seminaries in American history fell from being biblically Reformed, although they had plenty of volumes in their library, had authorization to grant degrees, had popularity and status among those wanting it, had promotion people to raise money, had financial endowments of impressive totals, had professors who were of world renown, and had stately buildings and grounds. A pastor friend of mine, in taking a New Testament course at one of these large seminaries, said in the study of 1 Corinthians 15 he seemed to be the only student who believed in the literal resurrection of Christ.

In the midst of trends to separate educational institutions from the over-sight and direction of denominations, God has preserved an important anchor: denominational control.

In the midst of a trend to change seminaries into training centers that are nondenominational in character, we have remained a seminary whose primary goal is to train pastors for the Reformed Presbyterian congregations throughout the world. We do this not because of who we are, but because of Whose we are. As God's children, we seek to build His Church.

One historian observed that the liberal churches have never had to learn how to "lay brick." They simply took over churches and institutional property built by biblically committed believers.

Woe to the Covenanter Church if it assumes that, having stood for biblical truth for 200 years, it is immune to the deadly virus of compromise. Students of history will recall the quick decline of the Presbyterian Church USA. Dr. J.G. Vos wrote:

> *In 1893 the Presbyterian Church in the USA suspended Dr. Charles A. Briggs from the office of ministry because he did not believe in the infallibility of the Bible. In 1936 in the same denomination Dr. J. Gresham Machen was suspended from the office of ministry because of his vigorous championing of the truths of supernatural Christianity. What was heresy in 1893 had become the dominant viewpoint of the denomination by 1936.*
> (What Price Co-Operation, 1944)

The Covenanter Church has worked to hold Biblical doctrines of infallibility, creation—not evolution, and purity of worship with its simple non-Episcopal form of worship: preaching the Scriptures, reading the Scriptures and singing the Scriptures. It has done so remembering how quickly compromises can occur.

The seminary must bow before God and humbly confess His graciousness in the provision of a denomination with a vision beyond its financial capabilities, a vision to provide a place to formally train her pastors and missionaries.

What a challenge to the faculty and seminary board members to support the Synod of the Reformed Presbyterian Church by their vigorous teaching and preaching when issues of compromise come onto the horizon of the denomination and surface in the courts of the church! (*Principiis obsta*—Resist the beginnings of evil things.)

Perhaps it goes without saying that God's Word is filled with commands to train others to lead. Paul makes it clear to Timothy to take what has been taught to him and to teach others so that they can in time teach others to obey. Training is both taught and caught. We read in Joshua 11:15:

> *As the Lord commanded Moses His servant, so did Moses command Joshua, and so did Joshua. He left nothing undone of all that the Lord commanded Moses.*

Moses so faithfully taught Joshua in his man-to-man seminary that Joshua left nothing undone of all that God had commanded his professor Moses. Elijah founded schools for training of the prophets (2 Kings 2:3, 5, 7).

On October 9, 1807, the Synod adopted the preface to the Constitution of the Theological Seminary. It sheds interesting light on the church's concept of the ministry and clerical education.

> *The living preacher should accompany the word of inspiration, in order to explain and apply its doctrines for the salvation of souls. . . .[I]t is the duty of every church to use the best exertions for procuring faithful men, who shall be able to teach others. . . .[I]t becomes necessary to provide a good system of theological education, for those who have it in view to preach the gospel of Christ.*

On January 7, 1959, the Pennsylvania Committee on Education approved the seminary charter. This was viewed as a major step in recognition of the Reformed Presbyterian Theological Seminary in academic circles.

Fourteen years later in 1973, following major building renovations and a high level of support from the denomination and the prospect of a fourth full-time professor, the state of Pennsylvania gave approval for the granting of the degree master of divinity. One of the state committee observations in making this decision was "the seminary's loyal support of the denomination ever since 1810 and the denomination's strong support for the seminary."

Students are unable to find in any other seminary in the United States the clear teaching on the Kingship of Jesus Christ over His three institutions—the home, the church, and the nation. Students are pleased to find a united faculty that continues to walk and teach the rights of Christ over nations and the place of dissent when the Kingship of Christ is ignored.

As you read the personal accounts of this book, you will find a thread of agreement and appreciation. The Reformed Presbyterian Theological Seminary has remained faithful to its anchor in large measure because of the strong teaching of the denomination whose Synod examines and elects the governing board and the professors.

The Reformed Presbyterian Theological Seminary is starting on its next 200 years. As we look at the continuing commitment to the Bible as the inerrant source of divine truth combined with a mandate to train men to be Reformed Presbyterian pastors, we must pause to ask how it continued through 200 years.

Will our Covenanter Church and seminary join the prediction of Joel Belz in a recent *World* magazine? "Given enough time, any institution, no matter how rooted in Orthodoxy will sooner or later slip away from its anchors."

As the fifth oldest theological seminary in the United States, we are celebrating the completion of 200 years of service to the Reformed Presbyterian Church of North America and to other churches. The source of fidelity does not come from fellowship with other seminaries that set forth the great doctrines of the Reformed faith. The source of stability in theology has not come from seeking world-renowned faculty members who do not, from the heart, teach the doctrines of the Reformed Presbyterian Church. No, the source of continuing strength for this theological institution is in the careful scrutiny shown forth for over 200 years by the Reformed Presbyterian denomination in the appointment of faculty and board members to guide the seminary to the high standard of biblical Reformed doctrines with the caring spirit of a loving pastor. This explains in large measure how the "turtle" got to the top of the six-foot post. It has been placed there by the continuing orthodoxy and careful oversight of the Reformed Presbyterian Synod.

As the crest of the seminary states, we are *Burning but Not Consumed*. May we continue to sense God's pleasure in allowing us to continue to do this for His glory for centuries to come.

ntinuing orthodoxy and careful oversight...

Donald W. Piper

Donald Piper emphasizes friendships throughout this chapter. Lasting student and faculty friendships characterize his down-to-earth description of his early seminary days. His was an unusually long seminary career, punctuated by missionary service in Cyprus and employment as a teacher. He charts the progressive change in the seminary from his first day there to his long service on the Board of Trustees, where he made new friendships. He served as pastor of the Seattle congregation from 1977–2008. He was elected moderator of Synod in 2001. Don and Boni Piper have been blessed with three children.

CHAPTER 6

Friendships

The bell rang, and I slipped into a seat in the middle of the classroom. A few seconds later, just as the professor began to greet us, another student skidded to a stop outside the door and slipped into the classroom to take a seat in the rear. He was in his pajamas. Thus began my first day in the Reformed Presbyterian Theological Seminary in the fall of 1965.

Having had no plans to attend seminary until a week or so before classes began, having never visited the seminary, having never had any preparation for seminary except perhaps the required Bible classes in my first two years at Geneva College, I really had no idea about what to expect. That day was unusual for me, not just because a student arrived in class in his pajamas, but also for other reasons. I was unused to a self-contained educational institution where unmarried students slept, ate and went to class all in the same building. I was unused to having a class with only four or five students. Although it was the sixties, wearing pajamas to class was pushing the envelope, and after the third time it happened, Dr. S. Bruce Willson, president of the seminary, gently encouraged the student to come to class fully dressed, which he did thereafter.

I was also unused to the curriculum. I had been a pre-med major in college. I still planned to go to medical school at Kansas University after a year of seminary. I was used to chemistry, physics and biology labs. Now I was taking Greek, Hebrew and church history. But that is what I wanted. The Lord had taken hold of my life a year before, and I wanted to learn as much as possible about the Lord, to whom I was in submission, and His Church before I went on with my life, and I believed that seminary was the best place to do this. I hoped these courses would give me the tools to know my Lord. I didn't absolutely rule out becoming a minister, but that was not my plan when I began seminary.

That fall four Reformed Presbyterian students entered the seminary: Bruce Hemphill, Dean Smith, Alan Nelson, and myself. No Reformed Presbyterians had entered the year before, or the year before that. There were a total of five students in our class, two students in the middler class and one in the senior class. So, while our class was small, it was the largest of the three, and it was the only one with Reformed Presbyterians in it. And of the four of us who began seminary that year only two—Dean Smith and Bruce Hemphill—were considering becoming ministers.

> ⟳
>
> *One great benefit of the seminary has veen to provide an environment in which those who live and study together forge friendships that last.*
>
> ⟳

The four Reformed Presbyterians who began that year became good friends. We have remained friends for the last forty years. One great benefit of the seminary has been to provide an environment in which those who live and study together forge friendships that last. Because of the time spent in seminary together, relating to other pastors in presbytery and synod meetings has been more than just business dealings or even "church" dealings. We work together not only as ministers of the gospel but also as friends.

My years of seminary training were a tremendous blessing in my life. I never went to medical school. I stayed in seminary for two years, then taught school in

Seattle for two years. I returned to seminary in the fall of 1969 with my wife, Boni, and we took a missionary training course together for a year before serving in Cyprus for over four years. Following our return from Cyprus, I taught school in Beaver Falls, Pennsylvania, for two years and then returned to seminary for a final time in the fall of 1976. I finished my course work in December and graduated in the spring of 1977. I think I may hold the record for being the longest matriculated student at the seminary.

The blessings over the years began in earnest that first fall. I learned much from my friendships and from the professors, who gave of themselves to teach and encourage us. Each professor had his own influence in my life.

Dr. Roy Fullerton was an example of hard work and loyalty. He cared deeply about his students. We were confident that he would always be ready to help in any kind of situation in which we might find ourselves. He taught by example how to care for people in a congregation.

Dr. Bruce Willson was always approachable and took time to talk to students. Only later would I realize how much Dr. Willson had to do with bringing academic respect to the seminary. His hard work for the seminary paid off. By the time I graduated the seminary was granting a master of divinity degree.

Through Dr. Clark Copeland I gained an understanding of covenant theology. Dr. Copeland had an uncanny gift for explaining the Scriptures in a lucid and systematic way that clarified my thinking.

Dr. Ken Smith brought to his class enthusiasm for saving the lost and an optimistic approach concerning the Kingdom. His excitement for evangelism combined with solid theology was contagious. Later on I had the privilege of serving with Ken in Cyprus where his love for the Lord and for the lost was as powerful and enthusiastic as ever. I observed that he was not just a teacher but also a doer.

When I returned to the seminary in 1976, Dr. Willson had retired and Dr. Stewart had become president. Dr. Bruce Stewart was the picture of gracious dignity. He radiated sincerity in his godliness. Under Dr. Stewart's guidance the seminary was officially accredited and began to reach out beyond the Reformed Presbyterian Church to attract people of God from the broader community. During his presidency the student body both grew and became more diverse. It has been a blessing to see the seminary grow to have a significant influence in the African-American church community in the Pittsburgh area.

During my absence from the seminary, Dr. Wayne Spear had joined the faculty. Not only was his knowledge of theology thorough and orthodox, but also he was a kind and gentle teacher. He also reflected a quiet wisdom that persuaded me that he would lead the church in the right direction. During my first years in Synod, I trusted Dr. Spear so much that I actually watched carefully to see how he voted in order to get an indication of how I should vote.

All my professors, along with the office staff, possessed a humility that was as instructive as anything they might have said. Besides being humble, they were all committed to the Word of God, to the Reformed Presbyterian Church and to the students. From the time I entered the seminary in 1965 until this writing, without exception the professors at the seminary have been exemplary in godliness, faithfulness and orthodoxy. No doubt the selection of professors by the board and by the Synod, and selection of office staff and librarians by the president, have been a key to keeping the seminary strong and orthodox.

Under Dr. Stewart's guidance the seminary was officially accredited and began to reach out beyond the Reformed Presbyterian Church.

My involvement with the seminary did not end when I graduated. In 1986 Synod elected me to the Board of Trustees of the seminary, and I have had the privilege of serving as a board member for twenty-one of the last twenty-two years. While I have been impressed with a number of fellow board members over the years, in recent years two men whom I believe have made the most difference to the seminary are Dr. William Edgar and Dr. Jerry O'Neill.

Dr. Edgar became president of the board during a time in which the seminary was facing a financial crisis and even the possibility of closing its doors. Dr. Edgar encouraged the board to take more responsibility in their role as trustees. He led by example. He himself was tireless in his work. His wisdom and his work in leading the board, along with his commitment to the Reformed Presbyterian Church, has been a blessing to the seminary that helped enable it to endure during a stressful time.

Near the beginning of Dr. Edgar's tenure, Dr. Jerry O'Neill was elected president of the seminary. He had been a friend of mine since we were boys in Kansas, so as I expected, working with him these last thirteen years has been a joy. A few years before he was elected president, the Synod had required that the seminary spend down its board-directed endowment. As a result, when he took office, the seminary was facing a financial crisis. Dr. O'Neill went to work on the budget with Dr. Edgar. Together, they worked us through the crisis. At the same time, both Dr. O'Neill's rapport with so many in the denomination and the denomination's desire to see the seminary continue resulted in heavy donations, which allowed the seminary to thrive once more.

God has been good to the seminary during the years I have been a part of it. He has raised up the right people for the right positions at the right time: from professors, to godly women in the office who were both capable and gracious in greeting everyone coming into the seminary, to knowledgeable librarians, and dedicated part-time teachers.

The board continues to work to keep the seminary academically sound, to maintain its heritage of orthodoxy as other institutions falter, and to keep tuition at manageable levels. We are pleased to see the Reformed Presbyterian Church continue to elect excellent professors and shower the seminary with its support. We seek to keep the seminary fiscally and academically sound. We desire to keep the seminary distinctively Reformed Presbyterian while continuing to appeal to students of other theological backgrounds.

I have enjoyed my forty-year relationship with the seminary, both in my years as a student and in my years as a board member. I have witnessed God at work in the church and in my own life through the blessing of the Reformed Presbyterian Theological Seminary as it has trained men and women to be His servants.

Walter W. Swartz

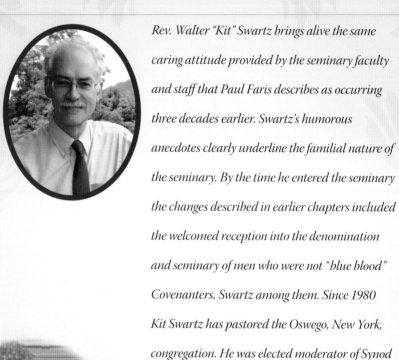

Rev. Walter "Kit" Swartz brings alive the same caring attitude provided by the seminary faculty and staff that Paul Faris describes as occurring three decades earlier. Swartz's humorous anecdotes clearly underline the familial nature of the seminary. By the time he entered the seminary the changes described in earlier chapters included the welcomed reception into the denomination and seminary of men who were not "blue blood" Covenanters, Swartz among them. Since 1980 Kit Swartz has pastored the Oswego, New York, congregation. He was elected moderator of Synod in 1999. The Lord has blessed Kit and Karen Swartz with three children.

CHAPTER 7

A Caring Family

When I look back at my experiences at the Reformed Presbyterian Theological Seminary (RPTS), I am struck by two facts: Our seminary endures by the grace of God, first, through its great love for and strong commitment to God's revelation in the Scriptures and, second, because of the seminary's loving care given to the students that God sends to this institution. The seminary is not only protected from the corruptions of idolatrous theological speculation but also, through its faculty and staff, there is evoked an affection in her students that has sustained her over the years by the many prayers and provisions afforded through the Reformed Presbyterian Church. I could cite numerous illustrations supporting the first fact, but it is the demonstration of the second fact that is on my heart. That is, that our seminary has continued in its spiritual integrity through its loving care for the students God sends.

All of us students could justly describe ourselves as "the students whom the professors loved." While there is a measure of sentimentality in the reflection, it is nonetheless true. Our professors cared for us as persons, as lambs in Christ and as future undershepherds of His sheep. Their purpose was to unite and conform us to Christ so that we and those who would later follow our teaching and example might truly be saved. I will, then, forever love my professors and our seminary, my only regret being that, for whatever reasons, I did not make better use of my opportunities while there. Still, God is good and in Christ, He made me sufficient in this as in all things He has called me to.

Examples of a caring faculty and staff abound. During my seminary years Dr. E. Clark Copeland, as dean of students, exercised a faithful pastoral ministry toward us. In one class, in an effort to encourage our reading habits, he required a report of pages read. My page numbers were low, and he asked to see my book. In interacting with the text at hand I had the habit of underlining and making frequent notes on the pages, thus causing me to read too slowly and too little. Dr. Copeland encouraged me to read more appropriately to the material, thus achieving a greater quantity. I cannot imagine this level of care in any other seminary.

Once I was ill, and Dr. Copeland came to my dorm room. Although he might have thought that I was being slothful, it became evident that he was sincerely concerned for me. An invitation to his home on a lovely autumn day was a simple example of his personal care for his students. Dr. Copeland's devoted care for his wife, Ethyl, impressed me not only when I was in the seminary but also many other times over the years. Though he was intelligent, accomplished and serious in his teaching, Dr. Copeland also had a wonderful sense of humor. After delivering one

of my first trial sermons in the chapel, I went to my room, changed clothes and ran down to the basement for the coffee break. Dr. Copeland met me and with a grin asked if I found preaching to be simply an artificial experience.

On another occasion, President Bruce Stewart was emphasizing the importance of humility for the pastor and contrasted that quality with the picture of a drum major proudly leading his marching band. I smiled because I had been a drum major myself in high school and college. Dr. Stewart, seeing my smile, remembered my service as a drum major and wondered if he may have offended me. At the end of class he immediately approached me with his concern. There was, of course, no offense taken, but I greatly appreciated his concern for me in such a small matter.

One of my most enjoyable experiences at our seminary was interacting with President S. Bruce Willson. A course that seemed to be a particular delight for him was Voice and Diction. Part of the instruction required our coming, individually, into his study to read aloud. He did not tell us beforehand what we were to read, but when I sat down, he handed me something by Dr. Seuss! Judging by the look on his face, handing me that book was one of the funniest assignments he had ever made. I was equally pleased, as I love reading aloud, especially something as challenging for the mind and mouth. We had a wonderful time together, each of us delighting in the joys of the Bach-like fugue of words and sounds.

Concerning the Bible Knowledge entrance exam, I am confident that I may still own the record for having one of the lowest scores ever on this exam. Scores, however, were never revealed to the students, but sometimes one just knows these things. Actually, much of the seminary instruction in my day was essentially remedial Sabbath School. Although some of my fellow students were Bible major graduates and light-years ahead of the rest of us, the professors challenged them without, at the same time, crushing us. Some of my professors' personal style and the nature of their subject matter caused them to paint a mural of the massive themes of Scripture and theology that was thrilling to the soul but often baffling to the mind. Dr. Copeland, for example, in his Old Testament classes, with his constant emphasis on covenant theology, exemplified this intellectual challenge. Dr. Willson's courses in church history were like this as well because his command of the subject was so vast.

So, given the considerable weaknesses of many of us students, the professors were kind and patient, but never indulgent. Their assignments were reasonable; their grading just. Typically, Dr. Renwick Wright always desired the best for his students, labored diligently to enable them to do well and then rewarded them according to their work. The professors always encouraged and admonished us when necessary for our good, but I do not remember a single rebuke, much less an outburst of anger. Not that a few outbursts weren't warranted!

The seminary staff, no less than the faculty, demonstrated wonderful care for the students. Mrs. Irene Caputo and Mrs. Sophie Sekowski served the seminary as housekeepers and cooks. In addition to providing a noon meal for the students, faculty and staff, these women, before they left in the afternoon, set up the evening meal for the dorm students. We would, then, simply serve ourselves and clean up afterwards. These ladies were very kind, treating us like their own sons. Once, Mrs. Caputo saw my old, stained, Bennington-pottery-seconds coffee mug and bleached it for me. Admittedly, the coffee tasted a bit strange for a few weeks, but at least I never had a head cold during that time.

The camaraderie among us students also served to make the seminary experience unforgettable. One evening, after supper, we set our chairs in a circle for prayer. Bob Hemphill was praying for God's blessing on Charlie Leach, who was shortly to preach a specimen of improvement sermon. Bob intended to ask God that Charlie would preach "clearly," but, as sometimes happens even to preachers, his mouth betrayed him, and the "cl" dipthong sounded more like "kw," with the resulting word sounding like an adverb synonymous with "oddly." I was sitting to Rob Miller's left and sensed his shaking and then heard his chair rattling on the concrete floor. Soon, everyone was overcome with laughter. Eventually, we composed ourselves and resumed our prayer time.

When the Lord was calling me to the pastoral ministry, and I was choosing a seminary, Pastor Ed Robson encouraged me to study at RPTS. I am thankful for this counsel, as it was clearly the best place to equip me for the pastoral ministry. I have had the privilege of counseling others in this same decision, and I have encouraged them in the same way and for the same reasons. No seminary, to my knowledge, prepares men for the pastoral ministry, especially ministry in the RPCNA, any better than RPTS. Today, I am happy to testify that the fruit vindicates the wisdom of the counsel that I received, for the Lord graciously continues to raise up faithful men out of our congregations to be trained in our seminary. It is costly for us to support our seminary, but it would be more costly not to, for we would have pastors lacking the RPCNA cultural context in their training; moreover, they would lack the kind of personal contact with professors and fellow students that RPTS clearly provides.

When I was a student, seminary board meetings reminded me of a warning from the wizard of Oz, emanating from behind the curtain, "Pay no attention to the men in the patio classroom!" Board members were always pleasant and encouraging, but I had little knowledge about what they did. Many years later, my serving on the board enabled me to thank God for those men who provided me with such a rich blessing at RPTS, and I thank Him now for those who continue this work.

I have observed three seminary presidents—Willson, Stewart and O'Neill—and I praise God for His wisdom and goodness in always raising up the right man for the right time. My strong concern is that we fully appreciate and support all those who serve the denomination at RPTS. It is easy to highlight weaknesses and to take for granted strengths and achievements. RPTS is a great treasure and blessing from God. It is good for us to reflect on this for the purpose of thanksgiving, and we should offer our petition that the seminary will persevere in maintaining its excellence.

Although these anecdotes may seem like a random collection of irrelevant memories, they all testify to God's grace sustaining our seminary not only through the priority of loving and defending His Word, but also by loving God through the seminary's care for its students. May our seminary always manifest obedience to both parts of the great commandment as it serves the Lord until He returns.

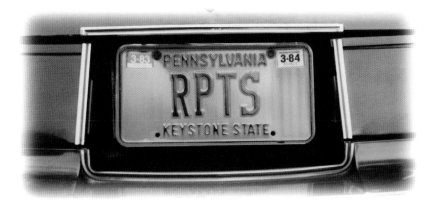

Brian E. Coombs

Brian Coombs represents the '90s generation of seminarians. Like Kit Swartz, a New Yorker and another newly minted Covenanter, Coombs describes the richness of the small seminary experience, resulting in a close relationship with his professors and the lasting friendships created in that environment. Brian is a graduate of Ithaca College in classical guitar performance. He received his M.Div. degree from the seminary in 1996 and became pastor of Messiah's Church, North Syracuse, New York, initially a satellite of the Syracuse congregation. He is Synod's parliamentarian and chairman of the Psalter Revision Committee. God has blessed Brian and his wife, Dorian, with four children.

CHAPTER 8

The Blessing of Intimacy

It was August 1993. I had just become a member of the Reformed Presbyterian Church of North America. This was the culmination of several months of study and a growing conviction that the Reformed faith was a truer expression of the Bible's teaching than that taught at my Charismatic church.

While anticipating membership in this new church, I was left with a great dilemma. For some time I had sensed a call to the ministry. My former church leaders had recognized such gifts in me months earlier. They had agreed to send me for theological training in the fall so that I might return to teach on staff.

Because of my change in theological conviction, however, I deemed it only right to halt my planned theological training at this time. It would not otherwise have been for the benefit of those who would incur the expense. And so, plans were put off. Had I misread the call of God? Had I thwarted it?

Being somewhat uncertain, I prayed, laying the whole matter before the Lord. I also sat under the preaching and counsel of guest preachers and elders in the Syracuse, New York, RP congregation. In the middle of August 1993, the guest preacher would be Dr. Bruce Stewart, then president of the Reformed Presbyterian Theological Seminary. And his announcement at the conclusion of the worship service was to encourage any young men who might be interested in seminary to speak with him afterward.

And so, hope renewed made the heart well. It also made for a speedy application and enrollment process for the imminent fall term. Once at seminary, however, my call was more and more confirmed of God, and my seminary experience very positive.

Certainly, there were negative aspects, like headaches from so much reading, and the need for twice updating my eyeglass prescription. There was also the constant challenge of finding more space for an ever-expanding book collection. But these were very minor—and endurable—in comparison to the major joys that came with growing in the grace and knowledge of my Lord and Savior, Jesus Christ.

The confessional standards and revered theologians were cited, but the Scriptures of the Old and New Testaments were always central.

While a student at the seminary, I was consistently exposed to biblical truth. It comprised the content of every subject and every class. The confessional standards and revered theologians were cited, but the Scriptures of the Old and New Testaments were always forefront and central. I appreciated the concentrated study of biblical *books*, in addition to the necessary regimen of hermeneutics, systematic and biblical theology, and pastoral studies. I also saw that even church history classes were, in reality, the unfolding and evaluation of how some doctrine or article of Scripture was being either advanced or denied. Careful training in the biblical languages gave me the necessary skills to work at a level underlying the accepted English translations, which I have found to be an invaluable asset, spiritually enriching, and a wise safeguard in the pastoral ministry ever since.

Still more, my exposure to biblical truth, having an appropriately academic color, was complemented with attention to and demonstration of a warm, biblical piety. How grateful I am that my training occurred in a climate of both theological and relational love and faithfulness!

Each professor was a humble, prayerful man of God who loved Jesus Christ. Each one sought to guarantee Christ Himself as the end result in the lives of students when all teaching was said and done. As one professor aptly put it, "True theology leads to doxology." Though human, and possessing their various idiosyncrasies, my professors were godly men—real men. They were husbands, fathers, grandfathers, neighbors, and friends; men in the world but not of the world. Even as we students regarded and approached them as professors, they dealt with us always as fathers; though we were but students, we were treated as future colleagues.

In addition to answering our theological inquiries, professors prayed with and for us. They showed a genuine interest in us personally, as well as theologically. We could (and did) go to some of them to share burdens. We asked and received counsel. Some would have us in their homes for meals or on social occasions. In these we saw that, in their public and private lives, what they taught they also lived.

Like most students, I was very much affected by Dr. Wayne Spear, who with wisdom, grace, and tact answered every question—the needless, the inane, the charged and the earnest— with the same gentleness and humility as he would his own child. His wife, Mary, also helped my wife, Dorian, and many other seminary wives, in their roles as our helpers. There was also the exuberance and friendliness of Dr. Edward Robson, who with his wife, Gretchen, impressed on my wife and me the place and practice of hospitality in the pastoral ministry. This was in addition to their many lessons from years of service, battle and blessing in the pastorate. These, in particular, stand out in my mind as men and women God especially has used in His continuing art of forming Christ in us.

The seminary experience for me, however, was more than classes and faculty interaction. It was here that key friendships were forged among the student body. In the kindness of God, many of these remain even now.

We would sometimes gather on weeknights to continue whatever theological discussions were left unfinished that day. How patient were our wives! On Friday nights, some couples and close friends would gather to talk, play games, and enjoy all manner of sweets and dishes the wives prepared. After this, sometimes, there would be the late night trip to Eat'n Park, just to insure that we slept in a bit on Saturday morning.

These gatherings had in them the seeds for even better things. Having been watered by God during and since seminary, we have now reaped a great harvest of love and ready encouragement for one another as we now rear our children and serve as pastors, though distances now separate us. I have been blessed through the seminary, but only because God has first made His blessing rest upon it.

The Reformed Presbyterian Theological Seminary has remained in existence despite some very difficult times. Its continuance is because of its maintenance of and conviction to teach Reformed and Presbyterian theology—even while training a student body of great denominational diversity, whose convictions may not align with the theology taught at the seminary. Allowing this student makeup, some of whom may not even be enrolled in preparation for the pastoral ministry, could be seen as running the risk of either diluting or compromising its own core values.

From my perspective, however, it has had the opposite effect. Not only has the seminary sustained its commitments, but also it additionally has led some students to a Reformed persuasion, and others into the denomination itself, either as members or, in some cases, pastors. If training at the seminary was limited only to men of our denomination, the seminary likely could not exist. Many men who have been enrolled as Reformed Presbyterian students sponsored by our presbyteries were not reared in the denomination. The last couple of decades have seen an influx of such men into the seminary. I was one. There have been many. I believe that such men have been one of the ways in which God has not only sustained the enrollment of the Reformed Presbyterian Theological Seminary, but also furthered the ministry of the church.

Looking back now, from the perspective of pastoring a small yet healthy congregation, I have come to believe that a large asset of the seminary, in addition to its historical-theological commitments, has been its smaller size. Herein was and still is a context for a theological and personal training of men for the ministry. How much of the pastoral ministry consists in relating to people! In this small context, I could know some of my professors beyond a mere classroom experience, so then I might truly remember those who led me, who spoke the Word of God to me, and, considering the influence of their godly conduct, caused me to imitate their faith (Heb. 13:7). This smaller context more easily allowed for establishing and building healthy relationships with future colleagues both my age and older. It provided greater focus for my cultivation as a servant and preparation to be a pastor.

We might be led by our culture to think that bigger is better and that size is proportionate to or commensurate with effectiveness. We would be pressed then to account for the fact that the apostolic circle, truly a "little flock," could "turn the world upside down" (Luke 12:32; Acts 17:6). It is not by might, nor by power, but by God's Spirit (Zech. 4:6), and He sometimes chooses to manifest His work in small things (v. 10).

In God's good providence we have a seminary to serve our small, but sturdy, branch of the universal Church.

I am not necessarily critical of larger seminaries. God has often used some large seminaries in ways equal to or beyond the Reformed Presbyterian Theological Seminary, but it is my observation that in God's good providence we have a seminary to serve our small but sturdy branch of the universal Church, whose fellowship we are blessed to have in the ministry of the gospel.

...fellowship in the ministry of the gospel

Richard B. Holdeman

In this chapter, Dr. Holdeman characterizes three men who influenced him greatly throughout his seminary career. Dr. Holdeman is a gifted pastor, joining Rev. Bill Roberts in Bloomington, Indiana; a professor of cellular and molecular biology at Indiana University; and, until retirement, a successful university ice hockey coach. A graduate of Yale, he received his doctorate in biology from Indiana University (1997), having joined the Reformed Presbyterian Church in 1991. He is a 2005 graduate of the seminary and has served on the seminary Board of Trustees since 2000 and as board president since 2005. Dr. Holdeman and his wife, Amy, are parents of three daughters.

CHAPTER 9

Three Hananiahs

Now it came about when the wall was rebuilt and I had set up the doors, and the gatekeepers and the singers and the Levites were appointed, that I put Hanani my brother, and Hananiah the commander of the fortress, in charge of Jerusalem, for he was a faithful man and feared God more than many. (Nehemiah 7:1-2)

In the days of Nehemiah, the Jews accomplished something incredible by God's grace—they rebuilt the walls of the city of Jerusalem. In human terms what they achieved was nothing short of amazing. Under Nehemiah's leadership the returned exiles were able to overcome the persistent opposition of their pagan neighbors, as well as some internal struggles of their own, to rebuild walls that had been destroyed decades earlier. Nehemiah rightly understood the basis for their success in this endeavor, saying, "And it came about when all our enemies heard of it, and all the nations surrounding us saw it, they lost their confidence; for they recognized that this work had been accomplished with the help of our God" (Neh. 6:16).

What was true in Nehemiah's day is certainly true in our day. Nothing great is accomplished by God's people without the hand of God. What is equally true, however, is the fact that God's work is usually done through the instrumentality of people whom He has gifted in particular ways to fulfill His purposes. As

I have contemplated the work that God has done at the Reformed Presbyterian Theological Seminary (RPTS), I recall seeing God's power clearly, but I also saw gifted people that He had raised up to accomplish His purposes there. Just as God called Nehemiah to lead the rebuilding project and then provided the faithful Hananiah to oversee the safety and security of the newly fortified city, God has also appointed faithful and God-fearing men to ensure the ongoing prosperity of RPTS. It was my profound pleasure and privilege to study under and work with many of these men. Accordingly, after I review a little of the history of my own involvement with the seminary, I will discuss how I saw God using a board member, an administrator and a professor as his "Hananiahs" at RPTS.

My first formal interaction with RPTS took place during the Synod meetings of 1994 when I, as a ruling elder, was a first-time delegate. At that meeting of Synod we elected a new president for RPTS. As a result of my participation in that election and of the fact that the newly elected president was my former pastor, Dr. Jerry O'Neill, I began to contemplate seriously the work of the seminary in training the pastors of our denomination. I became much better acquainted with the seminary after the summer of 2000, at which time I was elected by Synod to serve on the RPTS Board of Trustees. It was during this same time that God was working in my own life to call me to pastoral ministry. I began working on my MDiv at RPTS in the spring of 2001 and graduated in May 2005. My experiences as a member of Synod, as a member of the Board of Trustees, and as a student have given me a wonderful opportunity to see RPTS at work from many angles.

> ❦
>
> *I saw God using a board member, an administrator, and a professor as His "Hananiahs" at RPTS.*
>
> ❦

There is no question in my mind that the reason RPTS has been so successful at training pastors and has remained orthodox over such an extended period of time is because of the faithfulness and skill of those whom God had called to serve this institution. God has blessed RPTS with such people at all levels. I have chosen to highlight three examples of men who represent the many who have been used mightily in the work of the seminary and in my own development as a pastor.

When I arrived at my first RPTS board meeting in October 2001, I had no idea what to expect. What I found was a group of men committed to seeing the seminary honor God by training pastors for the Reformed Presbyterian Church, as well as equipping saints for various avenues of ministry in the broader church. The meeting was run with wonderful proficiency, and we actually completed our business about half an hour early. The members of the board had been organized into committees that did much of the work ahead of the meeting, so we were able to get maximum productivity out of our time together. The number of students at the seminary was increasing. The financial condition of the institution was much improved over previous years and was continuing to improve steadily. There was a tremendous spirit of camaraderie and excitement among the members of the board. A fellow board member told me, "The seminary board is a good board—you will really like being a part of it." Having had no other previous board experience with which to compare it, I did not at first understand fully what he meant, but I quickly found out. I also discovered that much of the enthusiasm, organization and efficiency of the board emanated from our board president, Dr. Bill Edgar.

Dr. Edgar came to the board in 1992 and was instrumental in the transition from retiring seminary president, Dr. Bruce Stewart, to current president Dr. Jerry O'Neill. Dr. Edgar, along with Dr. Stewart, played a key role in the seminary's move to Association of Theological Schools (ATS) accreditation. Dr. Edgar restructured the way the board functioned and ran board meetings that were the epitome of efficiency. In addition, he made improving the financial position of the seminary a top priority. By the grace of God, the seminary turned a financial corner and moved from the brink of insolvency to financial stability. As a member of the seminary board and as a student at RPTS, I have benefited from Dr. Edgar's leadership in countless ways. Even though he rotated off the board in 2004, it still benefits from the organizational work he did during his twelve years of service. God has indeed given RPTS faithful men—some in inconspicuous but critical roles. Many Reformed Presbyterian pastors who have graduated from RPTS can thank God for the work He did through Dr. Edgar.

While a good board president can have a tremendous impact upon an institution like our seminary, there is no question that the actual atmosphere of the institution is primarily a reflection of those who work in the building day in and day out. In many ways, the man who has had the most direct impact on the seminary in recent years is its president, Dr. Jerry O'Neill.

As a former member of Dr. O'Neill's congregation back in Columbus, Indiana, I knew him to be a gifted preacher and a committed evangelist. He was a man who loved his flock and who always seemed to have wise counsel for us. It was initially quite surprising to see such a gifted pastor leaving the pastoral ministry. Now that I have seen, both as a student and as a board member, Dr. O'Neill's ministry being multiplied through the pastors being trained at the seminary, I thank God that He moved him and his family to Pittsburgh in 1995.

God has used Dr. O'Neill's gifts of administration and development to move the seminary onto solid financial footing and to improve significantly its physical plant. His tireless work on behalf of RPTS has greatly increased its visibility in urban Pittsburgh and the greater Pittsburgh area and also in the Reformed community throughout the nation. RPTS has now hosted four highly successful conferences on the *Westminster Confession of Faith*, which have attracted participants from most of the major Reformed seminaries in the United States and from around the world.

One of Dr. O'Neill's truly remarkable contributions to the seminary was his work behind the scenes preparing the seminary for a major turnover in its faculty, which occurred in 2005 with the retirement of two long-time professors. He has been largely responsible for recruiting three of the four full-time professors as well as most of the adjunct faculty now teaching at the seminary. When one considers how critical the teaching faculty is to the mission of RPTS, Dr. O'Neill's work in this area has had and will continue to have a tremendous impact on the seminary's success and faithfulness to God and its mission for years to come.

> *A good seminary cannot accomplish its mission without committed men teaching faithfully in the classroom, day in and day out.*

In addition to these and other outstanding contributions Dr. O'Neill has made, he has, most significantly, also been a pastor to the men and women who study at the seminary. He told us in his Biblical Counseling class that he does as much if not more counseling as a seminary president than he ever did as a pastor. As a student, I personally benefited from his counsel on numerous occasions. As demanding as his responsibilities were, he was never too busy to talk. We can thank God for His ministry to us through Dr. O'Neill.

While I had the privilege of studying under many godly and gifted professors during my time at RPTS, the one who had the greatest impact on my ministry was Dr. Denny Prutow. A good seminary needs a good board and a strong administration, but it cannot accomplish its mission without committed men teaching faithfully in the classroom day in and day out. I can remember well Dr. Prutow's heartfelt prayers at the beginning of class each day. He often prayed that God would "forgive us our sins, which are *very* great." And when he prayed that, you knew he meant it. He put the grace of God in Jesus Christ before us in virtually every class meeting he had, and then he pounded it into us like there was no tomorrow. It made a huge impact on my thinking to see the focus on the gospel so clearly, no matter what the subject matter was. Whether he was teaching Homiletics, Old Testament, Pastoral Theology, Hermeneutics, or Doctrine of Worship, God's grace as manifested in

Jesus Christ was always the central ingredient. His approach was incredibly helpful in showing us the gospel in all of Scripture, in linking the New Testament to the Old, and in showing us the implications for our preaching and worship.

Dr. Prutow's effectiveness as a professor flowed from his sincere love for Christ and His Word. Because he had been a successful pastor prior to coming to RPTS, he approached his teaching as a pastor attempting to train other pastors. He was thus able to show us how the Scriptures could be used in ministry. This element is one of the key factors in making RPTS such a great place to study. Theology is not treated as some intellectual exercise engaged in for its own sake; rather, it is a vehicle to communicate the grace of God effectively to people who stand in need of that grace in our world today. Dr. Prutow epitomized the concept of a pastor training other pastors.

> *God is the one who provides for and protects His church, but He chooses to do that by means of particular people.*

His passion for the preaching of the gospel transformed my approach to ministry and is helping prepare the next generation of Reformed Presbyterian pastors. We can give thanks to God for what He is doing through Dr. Prutow's teaching.

Nehemiah put Hananiah in charge of Jerusalem because "he was a faithful man [who] feared God more than many." God is the one who provides for and protects His Church, but He chooses to do that by means of particular people. In my experiences at RPTS I have seen God use many people to make it a truly special place. In His providence, He has provided a board president like Bill Edgar, a seminary president like Jerry O'Neill, and a professor like Denny Prutow, faithful men who fear God. I thank Him that I have had the opportunity to benefit from His work through them.

Andrew R. Cooper

One of the most important changes to take place in the seminary over the past quarter-century is the steady growth in the number of students coming from the African-American community. Strongly evangelical, often already serving Christ's Church in local congregations, they provide a rich experience within the seminary family—diversity in the best sense of the word. Andrew Cooper is a 1982 graduate of the University of Pittsburgh and received his MDiv degree from RPTS in 2006. He is a respected pastor in the city of Pittsburgh, and a member of the seminary's 200th Anniversary Campaign Committee. Rev. Andrew Cooper and his wife, Debra, are the parents of two children.

CHAPTER 10

A Faithful Family

There were several things I witnessed that confirm God's faithfulness to the Reformed Presbyterian Theological Seminary (RPTS), allowing it to stay in existence during some very difficult times. One of the primary attributes of the seminary is its unswerving faithfulness to the Word of God. In being faithful to the infallibility of Scripture, RPTS is being faithful to Christ. One does not have to search long or hard in the Bible to discover that God honors faithfulness. In Genesis, the sixth chapter, God decides to destroy the inhabitants of Earth because of their wickedness. However, God says to Noah:

> *"But I will establish my covenant with you; and you shall go into the ark—you, your sons, your wife and your sons' wives with you. And of every living thing of all flesh you shall bring two of every sort into the ark.' … Thus Noah did; according to all that God commanded him, so he did. Then the Lord said to Noah, 'Come into the ark, you and all your household, because I have seen that you are righteous before me in this generation'"* (Gen. 6:18-19, 22; 7:1, NKJV).

Thus, God preserved Noah and his family during some very difficult times, honoring Noah's faithfulness, and declaring Noah to be "righteous before me in this generation." In much the same way, it has pleased God over the years to preserve and honor RPTS for its faithfulness to His Word.

The importance of a conservative, theologically sound, Bible-based seminary should never be underestimated. The training of pastors and other church leaders is a very vital ministry, and it has been my experience that RPTS functions as a ministry, not just as an educational institution. There is much caring, nurturing support given by the faculty and staff of the seminary. For example, professors are willing to avail themselves to the students in a variety of ways outside the class-room. Professors are willing to be flexible and work along with a sincere student who may be experiencing extenuating circumstances or who may need additional help. Because the seminary community is relatively small, there is a family-like atmosphere that is conducive to the overall welfare of the seminary student. The family of the seminary student is also included in the seminary community. Support for the wives of male seminarians—the Seminary Wives—along with other extra-curricular activities such as the Christmas party, various seminars, and banquets, provide for additional opportunities for learning and fellowship. The welcoming family-like atmosphere is perhaps another reason for the seminary's survival. In essence, the news gets out that RPTS is a conservative Bible-based seminary, concerned about the overall welfare of its students, faculty and staff. Most importantly, God does and will use a seminary that includes love in the curriculum. Therefore the seminary strives to erect biblical principles upon the only foundation that is sure, Jesus Christ. I am not surprised to see that this seminary continues to stand.

The sovereignty of God and the biblical tenets of covenant and Reformed theology have contributed the most in protecting the seminary from theological liberalism. All full-time seminary professors are members of the Reformed Presbyterian Church of North America. It is my experience that RPTS pastors/professors are a theologically tight-knit group. No doubt there are some theological variances in the denomination, but there seem to be no substantive theological differences among the faculty. Thus there is great theological uniformity among the professors, a uniformity that is a tribute to the denomination. There is something biblical and noble about being of one accord. In Philippians 1:27 the apostle Paul writes:

> *"Only let your conduct be worthy of the gospel of Christ, so that whether I come and see you or am absent, I may hear of your affairs, that you stand fast in one spirit, with one mind striving together for the faith of the gospel."*

I believe that from a covenantal perspective God sovereignly chooses and preserves whom He will, and what He will, to fulfill His sovereign purposes. Therefore, it is not a theological stretch to say that God sovereignly chose this seminary to fulfill His purposes in His kingdom for a time such as this. The people of God and the seminary community should be reminded of God's covenant faithfulness to Israel. In a time of spiritual declension, the prophet Isaiah prophesied about the coming of Israel's Messiah who would restore, comfort and preserve Israel from oppression and terror. Isaiah says:

> *"O you afflicted one, tossed with tempest, and not comforted; Behold, I will lay your stones with colorful gems, and lay your foundations with sapphires. I will make your pinnacles of rubies, your gates of crystal, and all your walls of precious stones. And your children shall be taught by the LORD, and great shall be the peace of your children. In righteousness you shall be established; you shall be far from oppression, for you shall not fear; and from terror, for it shall not come near you"* (Isa. 54:11-14).

What a very beautiful covenant promise! This promise, and indeed the whole chapter, comes to a magnificent crescendo of preservation in the seventeenth verse:

No weapon formed against you shall prosper, and every tongue which rises against you in judgment you shall condemn. This is the heritage of the servants of the LORD, and their righteousness is from me, says the LORD.

God does preserve His servants and their righteousness.

For me the person God used most to influence my ministry was President Jerry O'Neill. There are others at the seminary who have mightily influenced my ministry, but without President O'Neill's God-directed influence, I might not have gone to the seminary. Upon first meeting Dr. O'Neill I was very impressed by his warm, caring, friendly personality. Although he was a very busy man as the president of the seminary, he was willing to take a considerable amount of time to converse with me about the prospects of attending the school. During my initial interview with President O'Neill, it was like our souls were knit together in Christian unity. Using one of President O'Neill's words, our hearts resonated in our discussion that day. I knew that I was supposed to attend RPTS when Dr. O'Neill prayed for me right there in his office, asking God to guide me in my theological/educational pursuits.

I also have been blessed in some form or fashion by virtually all of the professors at the seminary. Professor Wayne Spear, with his vast knowledge of systematic theology and in his clarity in presenting this knowledge, was very impressive. Dr. Spear has influenced my understanding of theology, especially covenant and Reformed theology, which has benefited me personally and in my ministry. Currently, Professor Richard Gamble impresses me with his knowledge and humility. My language professors, Jonathan Watt, Edward Robson, and C.J.

...restore, comfort, and preserve

Williams, have played a significant role in my exegetical and theological growth, and therefore, in my ministry. The overall knowledge and wisdom of Professor Dennis Prutow and his practical tutelage in homiletics have been very valuable to my preaching ministry.

It is evident that I have had and will continue to have a very positive relationship with the Reformed Presbyterian Theological Seminary. Ironically, this positive experience has been bestowed upon a person who at one time did not know if the seminary experience would be the right theological "fit." Perhaps there are other seminaries that might have met my needs. God, however, has shown me that RPTS is not only the right "fit" for me personally, but is sharpening my ability to serve more broadly, and more knowledgeably, for God and His glory in His Kingdom on this Earth.

Sung Kug (Ulysses) Jung

One half-century after Bassam Madany arrived at the seminary another student came from half a world away. The description of his arrival in Pittsburgh closely resembles Bassam's. Ulysses tells us of his hesitation about choosing this seminary, but he then describes the great blessing he received from his professors. A graduate of Korea Open University (1995), he received an MBA from Hankuk University (1998) and an MDiv from Torch Trinity Graduate School of Theology in 2001. He is a 2004 graduate of the Reformed Presbyterian Theological Seminary. Sung Kug and his wife, Mi Oh, are parents of three children.

CHAPTER 11

An Unanticipated Blessing

When I was serving the Lord in a local church in Korea, I wanted to go to America to study. As I scanned the seminaries in America, my senior pastor strongly recommended the Reformed Presbyterian Theological Seminary (RPTS) where he had studied previously. In fact, he almost forced me to go there, emphasizing several advantages of RPTS, such as its traditional, Calvinistic Reformed doctrine, its teaching of exclusive psalm singing, and its wonderful, sanctified professors.

On my computer I found the RPTS Web site and read the information thoroughly. Everything looked fine. President O'Neill looked to be merciful, the school building looked beautiful, the class curriculum appeared reasonable, and the professors seemed well experienced. Two things, however, made me hesitant. First, RPTS provided at that time only the MDiv and MTS degrees. I had already earned an MDiv degree, so I didn't want to have another. The MTS looked a bit lower than the MDiv, because it simply reduced by one third the MDiv class hours and nothing more. What I really wanted to pursue was a ThM in Old Testament, but it was not provided by RPTS at that time. Furthermore, it seemed that there was no Old Testament professor who had a PhD degree in that area. The second thing that disappointed me was that the seminary looked so small. Perhaps I was not spiritually mature, yet to an immature young man, a small seminary didn't make me feel good.

After a long inner struggle, I finally decided to study at RPTS. The strongest factor that forced me to make the final decision was, without doubt, its sound evangelical, conservative doctrine. I strongly disliked liberal theology. I still do.

In February 2003, I was excited as well as a bit nervous, as my airplane was about to land in Pittsburgh. The new experience, the new challenge, and the different people in a foreign land filled me with a mixture of nervous and excited anticipation. In fact, this was my second visit to America. My first visit occurred when my wife and I honeymooned in Hawaii in 2001. It was in late February of 2003, if my memory is correct, that I came in the middle of the night to Pittsburgh. One of the Korean students gave me a ride, and he led me to the dormitory on the top floor.

> *The new experience, the new challenge, and the people in a foreign land filled me with a mixture of nervous and excited anticipation.*

I met President O'Neill, the professors and staff members the next day. The classes were not difficult for me since I had some experience with lectures in English in Korea. My Korean seminary offered classes in English since the purpose of establishing the school was to spread the gospel to the unreached people. All classes, therefore, were taught in English in order to train missionaries to send them to other countries. Furthermore, I had already taken most of the classes offered in the seminary; therefore, it was my second chance to study the same agenda. However, that didn't mean that I wasted my time, as most of my friends in Korea thought might be the case. They were worried about my plan, namely acquiring the second MDiv degree. I used the second chance to deepen my understanding and build my theological system on a more firm foundation. At the end of my study at RPTS I realized that I had a broader and more comprehensive perspective on theology. Furthermore, studying at the seminary not only gave me an opportunity to review what I had already learned at the previous seminary but also gave me a new perspective. Let me explain this in detail.

Unfortunately, I did not have many chances to take classes taught by President O'Neill. I took only one class, named Evangelism. But the time that I was with him in class had much influence on my philosophy of ministry. What Dr. O'Neill focused on for about half of his class hour was the *Shorter Catechism*. He asked the students to memorize it in its archaic English. Most of the American students suffered with it. Then, how much more suffering did a foreign student, whose mother language was not English, expect to have! Most schools in Korea use memorization as their educational tool, so I was quite accustomed to it. Memorization, however, in the archaic grammar along with the archaic English brought a greater challenge. I spent much time working on the assignment, accomplished it, and got a good grade. During that time I learned that the *Shorter Catechism* was sophisticated, was well organized, and conveyed sound doctrine. I could feel the tremendous endeavor that was made by our forefathers to establish firm doctrine. I am no longer able to recall the questions and the answers of the *Shorter Catechism* in its traditional form. Now, however, I am doing what I was taught by Dr. O'Neill. I am using the *Shorter Catechism* as a Bible study tool twice a week: once for the adult group who speak Korean only, and the other for the young adults who speak English.

When I shared my teaching plan with my colleagues (pastors) and asked for advice, most responses from them were negative, saying, "It won't work. Catechism is old stuff." However, I proceeded with it, and the outcome has been incredibly great. People love it, highly appreciating its value. Attendance at the Bible study is constantly increasing. Of course, I do not ask the laymen to memorize the *Shorter Catechism* in its question/answer form. Their spiritual maturity does not reach that level, so flexibility is needed. I interpret and convey the scheme of the catechism with the help of a great commentary.

I highly respect the two retired professors, Dr. Robson and Dr. Spear. In 2005 I drove from Chicago to Pittsburgh to attend their retirement service. I was quite blessed as I watched the PowerPoint presentation that night. I could feel their passion and love for Jesus and the seminary. They had spent many years at the seminary, teaching students. They had sacrificed their time and effort to keep the seminary from liberalism and to maintain its purity. When I consider how the seminary survived the tough times, and how the seminary has maintained its doctrinal purity over the generations, I think of professors like Dr. Spear and Dr. Robson, who have sacrificed their entire lives to study and teach the Bible and to keep the seminary strong against Satan's attack through a deep love for Christ and people.

Dr. Robson is the one who helped me open my eyes to see the Bible in its entirety. I think of his methodology as "intertextuality," which is the traditional Calvinistic and Reformed hermeneutic, as I understand it. The rudimentary philosophy of intertextuality is the idea that the Bible interprets the Bible. Dr. Robson taught students to interpret and to find the answers within the Bible scheme. The first time that I studied under him I was perplexed. After I understood his methodology I could handle Dr. Robson's teaching. I highly appreciated the methodology.

Without hesitation, I refer to intertextual methodology as I prepare a sermon or interpret a certain issue.

I took many classes taught by Dr. Spear. Among them, the most precious teaching was about Karl Barth's theology. Of course, I had learned about that theology at my previous seminary. What I knew about it, however, was superficial, so I had not realized how terrible Barth's theology was before I met Dr. Spear. He was the only one who made me open my eyes to see the reality of that theology. He sternly warned us of so-called evangelicals who used "check lists" to evaluate the validity of Barth's theology and were trapped by his dialectic. Eventually they wouldn't realize his intentional paradox at all, so whenever they met the intentional contradiction of Barth's scheme, they would "scratch their heads." In my experience there is no one who calls Barth's theology heresy as strongly as did Dr. Spear. I remember the answer from Dr. Spear when asked by one of the students in his class whether or not Barthian theology was heresy. His answer was quite impressive. He said, "I do not use the term 'heresy' as some of my students do, since the expression is too harsh. But in the case of Barth's theology, I do not hesitate to call it HERESY."

I had an opportunity to study the Eastern religions such as Buddhism, Hinduism, Islam and Confucianism. As I studied Karl Barth with Dr. Spear, I realized that Barth's dialectical system was quite similar to that of the two Eastern religions, Hinduism and Buddhism. Both of these religions use paradox such as "something is nothing and nothing is something," as their dialectical scheme. Hence, at the end of the class, I came to the conclusion that Karl Barth was more like a Hindu or Buddhist than a Christian theologian.

Let me conclude by saying that I saw the struggle that the seminary had due to the dearth of funds while I was studying there. I realized how much suffering and difficulty they had in order to raise funds to support and sustain the seminary. There are many millionaires in this country who support the secular universities and the liberal seminaries. It is sad that they do not have much concern for evangelical seminaries. A part of the reason for this is because the world is still dominated by Satan; therefore, we have to anticipate the constant struggle to survive in this harsh situation. The perseverance of the holy saints is still required. Second, RPTS is not a big seminary. It is relatively small. I believe that a part of the reason for this is because of the seminary's endeavor to sustain its purity from the virulent doctrine; this purity requires much sacrifice in the areas of financial support and quantitative growth. Finally, I am proud of being an RPTS alumnus. I do not hesitate to speak about my RPTS experience here at Trinity Evangelical Divinity School. I am thankful for all the faculty members of RPTS and am especially grateful to Dr. O'Neill and the two recently retired professors, Dr. Robson and Dr. Spear.

Rutledge E. Etheridge, III

Here Rev. Rutledge "Rut" Etheridge, III completes the
collection of personal testimonies running from the
1940s into the present century. Rut brings the collection
to a fitting climax, describing his years in the seminary
(2004–06) as both a time of transition and a sign of
God's providing continuity in the life of the institution.
Etheridge was reared in Baptistic dispensationalism.
He received a BA in Bible from Cedarville University
in 1999. Convinced of Reformed theology, he joined
the Second Indianapolis congregation in 2000.
He is presently pastor of the Providence Reformed
Presbyterian congregation in Pittsburgh. Rut Etheridge
and his wife, Evelyn, are parents of one son.

CHAPTER 12

Continuity in a Period of Transition

For the Reformed Presbyterian Theological Seminary, 2005 was a year of monumental transition. With the retirement of Dr. Wayne Spear and Pastor (his preferred title) Ed Robson, the sun had set on a combined forty-seven years of service to the seminary and its students. While every major transition in the life of an institution brings a degree of trepidation, the arrival of Dr. Rick Gamble and Professor C.J. Williams as full-time professors signaled the dawn of a bright new era in the seminary's history. In raising up these particular men for service at RPTS, the Lord provided teachers who embody the very principles that had proven so crucial to the survival and success of the century-spanning seminary. These principles have to do with the necessity and the nature of theological education.

Throughout its history, the Reformed Presbyterian Church of North America has deemed formal theological education indispensable to the life and well-being of the church. Fueled by this understanding, the Synod of the RPCNA refused to let its seminary die, despite decades of dismally small student populations. Without the fundamental commitment to training men for the ministry, the Synod surely would have removed the school from what appeared at times to be institutional life support. The church's commitment, however, to an educated clergy endured, and the seminary persevered in its work through stretches of minimal personnel and activity.

The denomination's insistence on the necessity of theological education was born out of its approach to theology in general and worship in particular. In order to understand and worship God aright, the believer must look first to God and to His Word, never straying in thought or practice beyond what God has prescribed in that Word. The regulative principle of worship, as it is referred to, presupposes the necessity of theological education. To worship God, we must know Him. To know Him, we must be taught from His Word. Therefore, the future leaders of the church must be equipped to lead God's people into the knowledge and worship of God. This need provides the impetus and reveals the necessity for seminary education.

Seminaries are often derided as spiritual cemeteries, and the kind of education they provide is considered the means of spiritual death. Some argue that time spent mulling over and debating ideas would be better spent outside the confines of the seminary doing "real" ministry. Sadly, this assessment may rightly describe the experience of some seminarians. However, its indiscriminate application to seminary education in general betrays a dangerous underestimation of the power and importance of ideas.

J. Gresham Machen, the great defender of the faith against theological liberalism, wrote: "What is today a matter of academic speculation begins tomorrow to move armies and tear down empires." In less epic terms, what starts at the seminary always ends up on the street. No law is ever written, no judicial decision ever rendered, and no moral decision is ever made in an ideological vacuum. The ideas we ignore today may prove to be our masters tomorrow. The prospective minister disregards the world of academia and the serious study of the Scriptures to the peril of his own soul and the souls to whom he will minister. High-level theological education is mandatory for the well-being of the church; those aspiring to be shepherds of God's flock must be taught how to lead and protect the sheep.

The history of RPTS is marked by teachers who have been solidly committed to providing the education so integral to the life of the church. Several of these men were so moved by the need for theological education that they dedicated vast portions of their lives to teaching at the seminary. The most recent example of such lengthy service is that of Dr. Wayne Spear, who served the seminary for thirty-five years. In 2005 Dr. Rick Gamble and Professor C.J. Williams had only begun their service at RPTS, but both men, in coming to the seminary, evidenced the same sacrificial commitment to theological education that marked their distinguished predecessors.

In heeding the church's call to teach at RPTS, Dr. Gamble left a prestigious teaching position in Florida and stepped away from ministry opportunities around the world. Most significantly, however, his coming to RPTS meant the uprooting

> *True theological education is an impartation of eternal truth so as to encourage and establish the informed, heartfelt worship of God.*

and moving of the most precious people in his life, his wife and five daughters. Professor Williams had taught part-time at the seminary, but in order to assume full-time professorial duties, he stepped down from the pastorate of Providence Reformed Presbyterian Church in the South Hills of Pittsburgh, a pastorate that could not have been dearer to his heart. Both of these men possessed the academic and ministerial credentials to teach or pastor elsewhere, but they chose to serve at RPTS. Their coming to RPTS spoke volumes about their commitment to theological education and in particular to the distinctive beliefs that have defined the seminary for two centuries. Along with their conviction about the necessity of theological education, these new professors brought an intense emphasis on the true nature of theological education.

True theological education is an impartation of eternal truth so as to encourage and establish the informed, heartfelt worship of God. This kind of education has not run its proper course until the intellect, affections and volition of the student have been transformed. The content of true theological education is the Word of God, and the goal of true theological education is piety. For Professors Gamble and Williams, this emphasis serves not only as a framework for teaching, but as an integral part of the content of the curriculum.

One of the first lessons that Dr. Gamble teaches his students is that the minister of God must never divorce doctrinal truth from the passion of the heart, for such a separation of truth and piety betrays a lack of true knowledge of God. In his lectures on systematic theology, Dr. Gamble becomes most excited when speaking about the believer's union with Christ and how that union is established practically in the life of God's people. Professor Williams brings the same emphasis to his classes. He persistently reminds his Hebrew exegesis class that the purpose behind such detailed contextual, grammatical and syntactical analysis of a

given text is the preaching of that text in a manner worthy and reflective of its deep truth. Only such preaching suffices to penetrate and change the hearts and lives of the people who hear it. These professors have taught their students what it means to truly know God. As the students move on to teach others the same blessed, galvanizing truth, the church will be substantially strengthened.

In bringing this kind of teaching to their students, Dr. Gamble and Professor Williams fit right in at RPTS. The integral connection between apprehension of doctrinal truth and heartfelt worship, between knowing and doing, between the "indicative and the imperative" is entrenched in the ethos of the seminary.

intellect, affections, and volition

That RPTS possesses this kind of environment is to a large extent because of its emphasis on hiring for its teachers men who have served or are serving in the pastorate. These pastors bring to their students the practical evidence of life lived in submission to the doctrines they teach.

Such teaching and modeling of truth has served to keep at bay the dangerous theological tides that threaten each generation of seminary faculty and students. Perhaps the most pervasive and deadly of these threats is theological liberalism, an ideological cancer which has been the bane of Christian doctrine and life for seminaries and entire denominations.

Theologically liberal churches are marked by their desperate attempts, as they see it, to make Christianity culturally relevant. These churches keep up with and emulate the social customs of their day, no matter how drastically those customs oppose Scripture. Frighteningly, many churches that on paper embrace traditional orthodoxy flirt with theological liberalism. While these evangelical churches reject much of the fruit of theological liberalism (such as the ordination of homosexuals to the clergy), they embrace the presupposition that is the seed of that fruit—namely, that the church must reflect popular culture's philosophies and trends in order to be relevant to those whom they seek to win to faith. This thinking, however, is entirely backwards. For it is precisely the church's refusal to compromise that makes her relevant, especially in a morally relativistic culture such as ours. The Bible is unchanging truth that transcends the rise and fall of kingdoms and cultures, and when the sociological and theological fads of the day have all passed away, the Word of the Lord will remain. By God's grace, RPTS has stood for two centuries on that immovable rock of truth. As a result, it has remained safe above the waters that have drowned so many other institutions during its lifetime.

In resisting the lure of worldly compromise, RPTS has also managed not to overadjust and fall headlong into the opposite danger: dead orthodoxy. Persistence in doctrinal, confessional rectitude is nothing more than a display of stubbornness if the full import of that doctrine is not realized in the lives of those who profess it. Christian love, the aim of apostolic teaching (1 Tim. 1:5), is both an indicator and a necessary prerequisite of spiritual health and safety for God's people. The appeal of theological liberalism is the alleged love and acceptance it offers. When true Christian love, founded upon true Christian doctrine, is present among God's people, then the illusion of love in other circles quickly fades, and its appeal quickly disappears.

The camaraderie that exists among RPTS's broad constituency validates this claim. There, people from divergent socioeconomic, ethnic and ecclesiastical backgrounds embrace one another as brothers and sisters in the truest and deepest sense. Doctrinal divisions exist among the students, but RPTS refuses to take the liberal approach to such differences. Rather than discounting the disagreements

and disdaining the doctrine at their center, the seminary considers the divisive issues important because they pertain to the Word of God. The seminary is, by design, a place where those issues are frankly and respectfully discussed. At the same time, it is a place wherein the doctrinal distinctives of its supporting denomination are taught without apology or compromise. In this environment of uncompromising orthodoxy imbued with the compassion that verifies commitment to that doctrine, true love and unity can exist among believers from different theological backgrounds. Students who disagree on church polity are united not only in believing that every word of Scripture is God-breathed but also together pursuing greater fidelity to biblical doctrine. This unity stands in stark contrast to the pretended unity effected by a willing ignorance of difficult doctrine, a unity forged in the false humility of an attempted Christian agnosticism. Out of love for Christ and love for each other, believers at RPTS search the Scriptures together that they might know more accurately the things of God. Such a relationship bespeaks loyalty first and foremost to Christ and His Word. Only when that loyalty is paramount can there be true love and unity in the body of Christ, and only when that loyalty is paramount can seminaries provide true theological education. Praise be to God, this kind of loyalty to Christ and to His Word is found in abundance at RPTS.

As the seminary faces the future, it gives me great joy to have seen the addition of two new professors, both of whom understand and model the necessity and nature of theological education. Their arrival marks the continuation of God's rich blessing upon RPTS and upon those around the world who benefit from its ministry. Truly the Lord has taken the seminary from strength to strength. If He does not return by then, may our King grant to RPTS many more centuries of faithful service to Him.

Maryln C. Black

The students who have shared these accounts of their seminary experience unfailingly refer to staff members, many of whom were (and are) women. Mrs. Maryln Black, assistant to President O'Neill following her graduation (MDiv) from the seminary in 2001, is also a graduate of Wilberforce University (1966). She has an MEd and a master's in public administration, both from the University of Pittsburgh, and is presently a doctoral candidate at Pittsburgh Theological Seminary. She has extensive service in the state Welfare Department. Maryln shines the spotlight on the women of the seminary, both as students and staff.

CHAPTER 13

The Women Who Stood

In the 200 years of the Reformed Presbyterian Theological Seminary's history, women have achieved many "firsts." In 1968, Kathryn Elliott (now Mrs. Ronald Stegall) became the first woman to earn the certificate of foreign missions, which enabled the Reformed Presbyterian Church of North America (RPCNA) to appoint her to a mission site in Cyprus. In 1987, the first women (Betty Green, Shirley Kerr, Pauline McClure and Marsha Petrarca) received the certificate of achievement. Laura Hill earned a master of divinity degree in 1990 and went on to be a youth leader in her church. In 2002, Barbara Buice overcame the obstacle of blindness to earn a master of theological studies degree and is now an instructor at the Community College of Allegheny County.

Today, the female student population is about one-fifth of the entire student body. Many of them already serve in ministries at their home churches and with Christian organizations. Some started their post-high school education after age forty and have struggled to orient themselves to academia. Some have full-time jobs and/or families and have struggled to balance school with other responsibilities. But each of these women has a deep love for Christ and the desire to do her best for Him. They will, we believe, go on to be great servants in the Kingdom of Christ. However, the "firsts" will always stand out as women who led the way for others.

There are also "firsts" in seminary personnel. JoAnne Luther, now Mrs. Bruce Martin, became the first seminary librarian in 1970. It was during her tenure that the two-story library wing was added to the seminary and dedicated in January 1971. Even I hold a "first" position as the assistant to the president. As the seminary and its mission continue to expand, other women will create new "firsts." Each of them, as well as each of those mentioned above, will have earned a mention in the annals of RPTS.

> *Each of these women has a deep love for Christ and the desire to do her best for Him.*

Yet, the women who deserve the highest accolades are the "women who stood." I am referring to those women who worked quietly behind the scenes and who dedicated their time and energy to the well-being of RPTS and its community. These are the women the RPTS histories mention only as the wife of a president or professor but who functioned as a pastor's wife to this small close-knit Christian community. These are the women who were (and are) the supporters, helpmates, and aides of the faculty from presidents to adjuncts.

Dr. Robert Copeland writes that before there was a Philadelphia facility, RPCNA ministers primarily received their training through private instruction, and that before 1814 at least seventeen of the twenty-six Covenanter ministers were privately trained (Copeland, *Spare No Exertions*, 11). A student attached himself to, studied theology under, and learned pastoral care from a mentor who was an experienced pastor. Often that student lived with his mentor's family. The culture of early America strictly defined the roles and duties of men and women in any household. Consequently, the mentor's wife would have provided for the daily needs of the student, usually a relative stranger, just as she did for the daily needs of her family. It would have been her responsibility to cook, clean and launder for the student. It would have also been her responsibility to be both a mother to the student and a role model of what a pastor's wife should be.

These wives set the standard for faculty wives, even today. I remember Gretchen Robson, wife of Dr. Edward Robson, sending fruit to the RPTS dormitory students. I remember Mary Spear, wife of Dr. Wayne Spear, coming to the seminary for a meeting and staying to clean the kitchen. I watch Ann O'Neill, wife of our current president, work to ensure excellent hospitality at special occasions. The tradition of caring for the faculty and the students has come down through the generations of seminary women.

Little is known or recorded about the "women who stood." So I want to share the little I know from personal experience with my readers.

Rachel George, who had previously held librarian positions at the Carnegie Library of Pittsburgh and United States Steel Corporation, came to the seminary in 1978 as librarian. Miss George continued in that position for two decades. She is an elegant lady whose bearing is straight. When I knew her at the seminary she wore a two-piece dark suit almost every day and her gray hair was always in a neat bun. I never saw her smile much although others who knew her well say she smiled all the time. She managed the library extremely well. I do remember being a new student and trying to find my way through the old library card catalog and hearing a voice say, "Let me help you." The

help lasted for thirty minutes and by its end I had an understanding of the catalog system and a full tour of the library facilities. Miss George took the time from her busy day to make a student comfortable.

I never met Sophie Sekowski, but her name still regularly comes up in conversations around the seminary. Sophie—no one ever calls her Mrs. Sekowski—was the housekeeper and cook from 1965 to 1997. A petite, slightly round woman, she was bursting with energy. She kept all four floors of the building clean for years. She cooked good, hearty, well-balanced, plentiful meals that everyone enjoyed. She used only dishes and silverware and for years did the dishes by hand. Sophie made all the cookies and treats for special occasions with the same ease that she prepared a lunch for the faculty and students or a dinner for the Board of Trustees. It is very telling that Sophie is still greatly missed.

Mary Spear (nee McCracken) is not only Dr. Wayne Spear's wife, but she also served as the seminary's secretary from 1978 to 1994. She is the mother of five children and, at last count, twenty-five grandchildren. Mary was the secretary before the computer age, which means that she typed on an old-fashioned typewriter with no auto-correct features. Her job was to keep the clerical side of the seminary running smoothly, and she did just that. Mary is also one of the humblest human beings I have ever met. She is never without a smile and is truly grateful for the very smallest kindness. I once sat a new and insecure student at a dinner table with Mary. The student left feeling important and loved.

I did not meet Roselyn Stewart, wife of Dr. Bruce Stewart, until I was an employee of the seminary. She is the mother of three sons and a daughter, and has fifteen grandchildren. Mrs. Stewart might be described physically as a delicate bird. Mentally, she is a giant. When Mrs. Stewart came to the role of the seminary president's wife she took on the role of the mentor's wife to the entire student body. It was Mrs. Stewart who oversaw the building just as if it were her home. Yet she is a gracious and kind woman who was instrumental in starting the Seminary Wives group to help the wives of seminarians become excellent pastors' wives. I know because I have never met anyone who did not love her. I know because I have seen her smile at me.

These are only four examples of the "women who stood." There are so many more. They are the women who helped the seminary achieve and retain its reputation for excellence in teaching, in rest, in peacefulness, and in unity of Spirit. They are the models for us who are charged by God to continue the traditions of RPTS.

Now let me also introduce the "women who stand" today.

Meet Carol Edgar, wife of John Edgar, the seminary's attorney, mother of four, grandmother of five. Carol is currently the seminary's secretary. A tall, thin woman, Carol never stops moving. She is a very friendly woman who opens her heart, her work world and her home to everyone. It is Carol who has the pulse of every aspect of the seminary at her fingertips. She should never be allowed to take vacation because only she has all the pieces in place in her head.

Meet Kim Backensto, wife of Rev. Bruce Backensto, pastor of First Reformed Presbyterian Church of Beaver Falls and adjunct RPTS professor, mother of five, stepmother of three, grandmother of two and stepgrandmother of four. Kim is the assistant to the director of development, Grant Van Leuven. She is the woman I go to when I need to make sure the details are correct. She is always willing to do the numerous little odd jobs around the seminary. I have no idea how she balances all her roles.

Meet our cook, Sheila Lewis, wife of RPTS alumnus Norman Lewis. Sheila has overcome difficult health problems and is a faithful member of the staff. She enjoys her work in the kitchen and loves to spoil the guys with her homemade desserts.

Meet Amy Troup, periodical librarian at the seminary, wife of Adjunct Professor Calvin Troup, who is also a professor of communications at Duquesne University, and daughter of Wayne and Mary Spear. She is the mother of four daughters. She also balances seminary life with her personal life of basketball and music lessons and all the things that come with four girls.

Meet Kristina Brehm (nee O'Neill), wife of Bob Brehm and the daughter of Jerry and Ann O'Neill. Kristy has overcome numerous difficulties to become the library assistant at the seminary. She loves to work in the library, which is a dream come true for her.

Meet Ann O'Neill, wife of President Jerry O'Neill. She is not so small as Mrs. Stewart, but appears to be when standing beside her husband, who is well over six feet. Ann is the mother of five, including a daughter now at Geneva College, and the grandmother of eleven. She carries on the work of the Seminary Women and gently watches over the workings of the community. She also has an almost uncanny ability to see into the heart of a person. She sends thank-you notes when a staff member does something especially thoughtful for another.

These are thumbnail sketches of a few of the women who stand behind and with the men of RPTS. I have been gratified to know many of them personally and to be inspired by them; therefore, it has been my pleasure to give you a quick view of them so that you may more adequately understand the important role that so many women have had in the history of the Reformed Presbyterian Theological Seminary.

JoAnn Smith

Maryln Black introduced us to the varied roles played by women in the life of the seminary. JoAnn Smith offers a delightful collection of stories about seminary life past and present, each, in one way or another, demonstrating her love for her church and its seminary. Mrs. Smith, daughter of Scott Boyle and granddaughter of long-time missionary Dr. Sam Boyle, moved often with her Navy family, finally settling in the Westminster, Colorado, congregation where she met her husband, David Smith. She was a seminary wife (1999–2002), and now serves with her pastor husband in the Orlando, Florida, congregation. JoAnn and David Smith are parents of three children.

CHAPTER 14

Stories from a Seminary Wife

For 200 years the Reformed Presbyterian Theological Seminary has been impacting lives of seminarians, yes, but also the lives of those around them. I am glad to relate here how I have benefited from our seminary as the grandchild of a Reformed Presbyterian pastor/missionary, the wife of a Reformed Presbyterian pastor, and as a lifelong congregant shepherded by our seminary's graduates. It is for these reasons that I have an increasing appreciation for the invaluable service the seminary provides as it seeks to prepare men and women for the Lord's work.

As I was growing up in the Westminster Reformed Presbyterian Church in Westminster, Colorado, I was greatly blessed by the ministry of my pastors. Under their preaching and teaching, I came to know the gospel and to love the doctrines of the church. I marveled at their knowledge and frequently questioned them on matters of the faith. I was never disappointed. It wasn't until later that I fully appreciated the role the seminary played in training these men.

Along with the ongoing ministry I received from my pastors, I was also affected by the summer interns from the seminary that my church and other congregations in the presbytery often hosted. These interns took active roles in the children's and young people's ministries at our church and at presbytery events. These men and their wives influenced me greatly as I saw their excitement about the job they had come to do, their willingness to spend time with the youth, and their openness about

their faith. I saw that it was possible to be "cool" and fun and yet still be a Christian who was not afraid to speak of one's faith.

Before being used mightily for the Lord in both hemispheres, my grandfather, Dr. Samuel E. Boyle, graduated from RPTS. He was well known for always having a story to tell on any topic and the seminary was no exception! It seems that one day in his first year in the seminary, my grandfather would also be used mightily to break in the new president and professor of Hebrew and Greek, Dr. R.J.G. McKnight. Dr. McKnight knew of Grandpa's propensity to draw cartoons but did not want to become the subject of one. Grandpa was undaunted. His solution was to draw his cartoon on the back of an exam, knowing that Dr. McKnight would see it but would be unable to throw it away. After grading the paper Dr. McKnight reluctantly returned the exam and cartoon. That cartoon then increased in popularity. Its fame spread, and eventually it was framed and displayed in the home of Rev. Hugh and Alison Blair in Ireland and published in Dr. Robert M. Copeland's book, *Spare No Exertions: 175 Years of the Reformed Presbyterian Theological Seminary.* I discovered recently that Grandpa still managed to receive a B+ on his exam.

In the early 1990s, another seminary president shouldered an entirely different kind of burden of his office. The seminary was experiencing financial difficulties, and during this time President Bruce Stewart visited my church. I remember Dr. Stewart emphasizing the importance of the institution and the critical need for a place to train the future pastors of our denomination. I was affected by his warning that without solid, biblical training, the future of our denomination was in jeopardy. I realized that I had been taking for granted the work the seminary was doing. This was when I was motivated to support the seminary in a much greater way and to pray for it more fervently in light of these new insights. The 40/40 Support Plan was a great annual reminder of the seminary's continuing need for financial assistance and prayer.

In 1997, after I had married David Smith, a member of the Westminster congregation, our giving to and receiving from the seminary took a much more personal turn. David had a great love for the study of God's Word, and we eagerly agreed that RPTS would be the ideal place to further develop this passion. In 1999, we moved into the "Old Seminary Apartments" on Penn Avenue, right next door to the seminary. This enabled both of us to be very involved in seminary life. David was blessed by his studies and by the instruction, assistance and encouragement received from his

> *The Lord was using the seminary to develop the man who was to be my pastor.*

professors. During the three years we spent in Pittsburgh I saw him grow in his love for and knowledge of Jesus Christ, cultivate friendships, mature in leadership, and begin to transform from a struggling seminary student to the confident preacher he is today. The Lord was using the seminary to develop the man who was to become my pastor.

David was an earnest student; he studied long and hard, and because of this our time at the seminary became a life of very little money and even less free time. Therefore, David and I seldom had an opportunity to enjoy Pittsburgh's cultural attractions together. On one occasion, however, my parents gave us center third row tickets to *The Nutcracker*. Despite the approaching exams, we arranged for a babysitter, and off we went. After finding our comfortable seats behind the orchestra pit we relaxed and I began to enjoy the show. But David very quickly fell asleep! Although not in the manner we had expected, the ballet provided David with a much-needed rest from the weeks of continuous studying!

As a seminary wife, I had the privilege of auditing classes. I was especially challenged and rewarded by the class entitled Spiritual Development taught by President Jerry O'Neill, in which I had the opportunity to memorize a portion of the *Shorter Catechism*, meet on a regular basis for prayer with a fellow seminary wife and auditor, and read books that I would not have been aware of nor had the determination to study on my own. While taking just one class at a time without the pressure of earning a grade, I understood in a greater way the tremendous effort my husband and his fellow students were putting forth! I was also able to attend chapel where I was blessed by hearing God's Word preached and His Psalms sung on a regular basis.

Another wonderful part of seminary life for me was the fellowship among the wives of the seminarians. We spent time together at the seminary, in classes, at church, in Bible studies, and in each others' homes. Our children played together, we were pregnant together, and as a result of the many hours of their studying, we missed our husbands together. We developed friendships with one another that will last a lifetime. The highlight of our time together came at the monthly Seminary Wives meetings led by professors' wives, chiefly Ann O'Neill, Mary Spear and Gretchen Robson. We were, however, affectionately referred to as "Seminary Widows."

At these meetings we received valuable insights designed to prepare each of us for the future as a pastor's wife. Our meetings covered many topics such as hospitality, responsibilities of a pastor's wife, struggles unique to a pastor's wife, confidentiality, how to support our husbands, training of our children, and finances.

Hospitality was a topic that I was especially interested in. I had come to recognize the importance of it but was feeling inadequate and ill prepared to do it. One principle I learned and am continually grateful for is this: "Hospitality is not primarily about the food or the tidiness of my home; rather the goal of hospitality is to facilitate fellowship and to build relationships." On one occasion, Rev. Ray Joseph and his wife, Alice, were in Pittsburgh at the same time as our monthly Seminary Wives meeting. Alice graciously agreed to speak to our group about her experience as a pastor's wife. As part of her talk, Alice spoke of the likelihood that we would be asked to entertain guests on short notice and of the importance of being prepared. She warned us of the temptation to spend a portion of the Sabbath morning worship service planning a menu for the unexpected visitors in attendance. I heard her warning but nevertheless have succumbed to the temptation on more than one occasion!

We heard from pastors and their wives, professors and their wives, and others qualified to deliver relevant information. There have been countless times since my husband assumed the role of a pastor that I have utilized information received at these meetings. I have often thought to myself, "Oh, yes! They said this would happen!"

My experience with the seminary, therefore, has undergone a progression from an admirer of the pastors the seminary has produced, to a deliberate supporter of the seminary's work, and finally to my role as a direct participant in my husband's ministry. I am grateful to be a recipient of the benefits provided by the seminary as it faithfully proclaims the inerrancy of Scripture, the Reformed faith, and the Kingship of Christ while training pastors for the ministry of the gospel.

Wayne R. Spear

The students from the 1940s to the present have spoken. We have learned about the significant role that women have played in the life of the seminary as students and staff and students' wives. Dr. Wayne Spear, a student himself in the fifties and professor of systematic theology (1970–2005) now describes his relationship with the seminary, emphasizing its growth and present strength. Before coming to the seminary Dr. Spear served as pastor of the Lake Reno (Glenwood, Minnesota) and San Diego congregations. He was elected moderator of the Synod in 2002. Wayne and Mary Spear are parents of five children.

CHAPTER 15

A Faculty Member's Testimony

I sometimes responded to a historical question from a seminary student with the words of a lawyer: "I don't know the answer to any question beginning with 'Why?'" I have that difficulty in mind as I reflect on what factors, under God's merciful providence, have contributed not only to the survival but also to the flourishing of the Reformed Presbyterian Theological Seminary (RPTS). My frame of reference is my time at the seminary: three years as a student, 1957–1960, and thirty-five years on the faculty, 1970–2005.

The first factor that comes to mind is the long-term positive response of the Synod and the Reformed Presbyterian Church to the initiatives of Dr. S. Bruce Willson and the seminary board. When Dr. Willson came as president in 1953, the seminary was only marginally an academic institution, with a minuscule library, an aging building, an informal curriculum, and little, if any, record-keeping. Dr. Willson set about to bring both structure and vitality to the seminary's operation. The Synod approved a new constitution, with a more deliberate and thoughtful process of electing professors. The goal was set of gaining approval from the Pennsylvania Department of Education for granting degrees. Pennsylvania's standards were high. Achieving the goal would require substantial improvements in academic standards, finances, library and faculty qualifications.

To upgrade faculty preparation, the Synod accepted board recommendations

that sent several men to graduate school at Synod expense. Clark Copeland, Bruce Willson, Duncan Lowe and I were thus given help in academic preparation.

With the generous support of the church, two major improvements of the seminary building were completed under Dr. Willson's leadership: a general renovation in 1960 and the addition of a library wing in 1970. Significant improvements have continued in recent years under Jerry O'Neill's presidency. These brick-and-mortar changes have made it easier to recruit students from other churches in Pittsburgh and beyond.

Meanwhile, Dr. Willson and the board were patiently pursuing degree-granting authority. After twenty years, that effort was rewarded. An evaluation team visited the seminary, and made a positive recommendation. I still remember the tension on the day Dr. Evans came to the seminary and met with the faculty. He laid a letter from the Secretary of Education on the old desk in the library, and proceeded to discuss several things that needed further improvement. Then, to our great relief and joy, he handed over the letter that granted the seminary the right to offer the master of divinity degree.

The ability to offer a graduate degree greatly increased the appeal of the seminary to Reformed and evangelical believers in western Pennsylvania and beyond. Reformed Presbyterian presbyteries were willing to accept ministerial candidates from their own seminary, but governing bodies in other churches desired the objective validation that a graduate degree provided. The size of the student body began to grow, extending the ministry of the seminary and also increasing revenue from tuition.

Providentially, in 1958 there was a merger of two other Presbyterian seminaries in Pittsburgh: Western and Pittsburgh-Xenia seminaries were joined to form Pittsburgh Theological Seminary. Prior to that merger, Pittsburgh-Xenia had been a substantially evangelical seminary, led by men like Addison Leitch and John Gerstner. Pittsburgh Seminary largely adopted the liberal theology of Western Seminary. RPTS became the only seminary in the city deeply committed to the full trustworthiness of Scripture and to the Westminster Standards. This attracted increasing numbers of students, not only from NAPARC churches, but also from other evangelical churches as well.

The ability to offer a graduate degree greatly increased the appeal of the seminary to Reformed and evangelical believers in western Pennsylvania and beyond.

Significant numbers of African-American students, many of them already pastors, came to us when they learned that we believed in and taught the Bible. Leading men in that community, such as Dr. LeRoy Walker, Alvin Coon, and Maurice Doss, not only studied with us but also recommended the seminary to others. It has been an enriching experience to have fellowship with these brothers and sisters, to find how much we share in Christ despite our doctrinal and cultural differences.

The effort to enhance the seminary's academic quality continued under President

Bruce Stewart. The seminary was granted accreditation from the Association of Theological Schools in 1994. This action strengthened our ability to recruit students.

Another factor contributing to the growth of the seminary has been cooperation with Geneva College. Geneva's Center for Urban Biblical Ministry and Degree Completion Program have enabled students who are in pastorates or are working to get academic training. Because they become familiar with the building and get acquainted with seminary faculty and staff, a good number have subsequently enrolled in the seminary.

One factor that has to some extent distinguished RPTS from other seminaries is our strong emphasis on preparation for pastoral ministry. There has been an unwritten, but consistently observed rule that full-time professors should have significant experience as pastors of congregations. Many of our students are already active in ministry and appreciate classroom instruction with a pastoral and practical focus.

When one surveys the history of theological education, a disappointing trend is apparent. Many seminaries, once known for their commitment to the authority of Scripture and other foundational tenets of the Christian faith, have come over the years to embrace theological liberalism in its various forms. By God's amazing grace, the Reformed Presbyterian Theological Seminary is an exception to that trend. With a history of two centuries, the seminary has continued to teach the doctrines of historic Christian orthodoxy with vigor. This is the Lord's doing, and it is marvelous in our eyes!

In my view, one of the ways in which the Lord has worked is through the continuing denominational control of the seminary. The seminary's constitution is subject to direct approval by the Synod of the Reformed Presbyterian Church, and full-time professors are elected by the Synod. This in itself would not assure

the continuing soundness of the seminary, if the church were drifting. Again by God's grace, however, the church and its Synod have remained orthodox and have made sure that the seminary where many of its pastors are trained reflects the theology of the sponsoring denomination. Moreover, that control has been backed up by generous financial support.

By God's grace, the church and its Synod have remained orthodox and have made sure that the seminary reflects the theology of the sponsoring denomination.

Those who do not know the history of the Reformed Presbyterian Church well sometimes say that there was a time in the 1930s and 1940s when the church had drifted into liberalism and only more recently has come back to the Reformed faith. I do not agree with that assessment. In the period in question, it is true that the Covenanters shared some societal concerns and goals with the adherents of the so-called "Social Gospel." The Social Gospel movement, however, had substituted a program of social reform for the supernatural, saving gospel. The Reformed Presbyterian Church always held to the real gospel. The *Declaration* and *Testimony* of the church clearly stated the historic Christian faith and was strongly adhered to by the officers and members. The *Westminster Shorter Catechism* was central in the training of the youth of the church. There was perhaps some lack of theological discernment, but I believe the church as a whole remained committed to the Reformed faith.

That commitment was strengthened in the latter part of the twentieth century by the influence of men like Sam Boyle, Lester Kilpatrick, J.G. Vos, and S. Bruce Willson. Such men cultivated fellowship with leaders in other Reformed denominations and sought to strengthen the church's historic stance. Dr. Vos's

Blue Banner Faith and Life was especially influential. All the seminary faculty that I have known have stood firmly for "the faith once delivered to the saints."

In recent years, helpful influence from other Reformed bodies has continued. Dr. Bruce Willson was personally acquainted with leaders of the Presbyterian Church in America in the period when that denomination was founded. Dr. Bruce Stewart has been active in the work of the North American Presbyterian and Reformed Council for many years. Several recent faculty members have been affiliated with Westminster Theological Seminary in Philadelphia. Professors Duncan Lowe, Ed Robson, Tom Reid, and I were students there; Professor Rick Gamble has served on the Westminster faculty. These associations have helped the seminary maintain its Reformed identity and commitment.

Conservative colleges and seminaries face a subtle but powerful temptation to strive for acceptance in the broader intellectual community in which they operate. But the gospel is foolishness in the eyes of the world's wisdom (1 Cor. 1:18-21). So a strong commitment to the doctrines of Scripture will always be damaging to an institution's desire for academic acceptance. Because of its small size and the faculty's commitment to teaching rather than to research and writing, I believe this temptation has not influenced RPTS in the way it has some other institutions.

There have been many persons who have shaped my own ministry at the seminary. Those who have been most influential are, quite naturally, those who were my colleagues in the earlier years of my teaching: Bruce Willson, Clark Copeland, Bruce Stewart and Renwick Wright.

Dr. Bruce Willson was my favorite teacher during my student years. He was an effective communicator; it was not hard to pay attention in his classes. He transmitted to me his love of exploring the thought of Christian writers of the past, particularly John Calvin and Abraham Kuyper. During my student preaching, I always sought out his face; he interacted visibly, and his expression was always encouraging. He recruited me for service at the seminary; when I declined the first invitation, he traveled to San Diego and applied his personal influence to lead me to change my mind. It was a great privilege to serve alongside him at the seminary.

Dr. Clark Copeland was briefly my seminary teacher, when he came to teach a short course on missions. I remember his godly influence on the students as he lived in the seminary building and shared our meals. He had an amazing capacity for work, in the early years teaching both Old and New Testament courses. I marvel at his grasp of the Scriptures and of their unifying theme, the covenant. For several years we commuted together to the seminary from Gibsonia, and those were wonderful times of biblical, theological and spiritual conversation.

Dr. Bruce Stewart had been a fellow pastor with me in the Pacific Coast Presbytery, and I was delighted when he came to the seminary. He has been, over the years, one of my closest friends. I admire his diligence; whatever he does, in speaking or in committee work, he is thoroughly prepared. Yet he almost never

appears to be rushed. He has a gentle spirit; but he is a strong man, committed to Scripture and to the church.

Dr. Renwick Wright shared with his students his love for the New Testament in the original language; perhaps they learned to pronounce Greek with an Irish accent! He came to the seminary after long and effective pastoral ministry in Ireland and America, and modeled well how to combine literate, challenging preaching with the caring heart of a pastor. When he said, "We will pray for you," I always knew that it was no platitude; he and his wife, Maureen, would really pray.

For these fellow-laborers and for more recent colleagues, I am profoundly grateful to God. The seminary is what it is today primarily because of the godly men who have taken seriously their task of passing on to the rising generation the riches of the Scripture and of the historic Christian faith. This they did because they loved Christ and the gospel and wanted to share God's grace with their students.

...the caring heart of a pastor

Thomas G. Reid, Jr.

An educational institution's library ranks high on the list of essential assets. Even in the time of electronic advances, the presence of the printed word is invaluable. Following Dr. Spear's assessment of faculty strength, Librarian Tom Reid here sketches the development of seminaries and the parallel development of seminary libraries, particularly the remarkable expansion of the Reformed Presbyterian Theological Seminary library. Reid, a graduate of Westminster Theological Seminary, Philadelphia, pastored the Creevagh RP Church in Ireland and the Quinter, Kansas, congregation. He was librarian at Reformed Theological Seminary, Jackson, Mississippi, before assuming his present position as seminary librarian in 1996. Tom Reid and his wife, Genevieve, are parents of two children.

CHAPTER 16

The Seminary's Best Kept Secret

The development of theological education in North America has occurred in four phases. During the first phase, essentially the colonial period, ministers were trained by obtaining an undergraduate degree, either at an Old World university or in one of the fledgling institutions of higher education founded in North America. These men then served as interns with older ministers in order to complete their preparation for the ministry.

Dissatisfaction with this scheme soon developed for various reasons, from the tendency of young men to reproduce the strengths and especially *weaknesses* of their individual mentors, to the desirability of having men training together for their future ministries, with the inevitable give-and-take—academic, spiritual and practical—that such a setting involves. Thus, in the second phase, one or two prominent ministers were set apart to prepare small groups of men for the pastoral ministry in specific locations. Following the Civil War, these small institutions, hardly bigger or better than what they had replaced, in the third phase morphed into legitimate institutions of higher education, as their faculties grew in number, professors earned higher degrees (often in Europe), facilities were developed, and finances stabilized. In the fourth and final phase, beginning between the two World Wars of the twentieth century, theological seminaries became multi-faceted educational powerhouses, training men and eventually women for various forms of ministry in varied denominational, interdenominational and para-church settings.

The development of the libraries of these theological seminaries grew in four great epochs as well, corresponding to the broader developments in theological education. The early libraries were simply the mentoring pastor's personal collection. In the second phase, they were not much more, but at least were supplemented by a few of the outstanding works that the professor(s) did not own. By the third phase, special rooms were being set aside to house growing collections now far beyond the typical scholarly pastor's library in size; a seminary professor was, perhaps reluctantly, assigned to keep watch on the shelves slowly filling up with resources collected in an organized way. In the fourth phase, libraries were housed in imposing edifices, their collections cataloged using the Union Theological Seminary (of New York City) scheme (later replaced in most cases by the Library of Congress Classification), with professional librarians running the whole operation.

> *At its founding in May 1810, RPTS was an itinerant, one-professor affair, occasionally suspended, until it settled permantly in Pittsburgh, Pennsylvania, in 1856.*

For those familiar with the history of the Reformed Presbyterian Theological Seminary (RPTS), the outlines above should sound familiar, for they are the story of the seminary and its library. Early on, Reformed Presbyterian ministers were trained haphazardly in North America, although as early as 1786 there was the option of studying at the Scottish Reformed Presbyterian Seminary. At its founding in May 1810, the Reformed Presbyterian Theological Seminary was an itinerant, one-professor affair, occasionally suspended, until it settled permanently in Pittsburgh, Pennsylvania, in 1856, and a second professor was added. What we know of the library—and that is almost nothing—suggests that it was little more than the professor's

collection and then some. Dr. Robert Copeland's *Spare No Exertions: 175 Years of the Reformed Presbyterian Theological Seminary* makes virtually no mention of the library until Part IV, which covers the years 1953 to 1985, and that lacuna does not stem from any lack of research on the part of Dr. Copeland. From 1856 until Dr. S. Bruce Willson was appointed president in 1953, the library grew slowly, gradually spreading out into several rooms in the mansion purchased to house the seminary in 1924. The collection was uncataloged, arranged by subject on the shelves, and not considered a strong point in the seminary's ministry.

Dr. Willson's arrival ushered in a period of modernization for the seminary and its library that has led to breathtaking changes over the past half-century. Having lagged considerably behind other institutions, the seminary eventually caught up with them. Consider the growth of the library's physical setting: A two-story library wing was added in 1970; it was originally intended to be one floor, but the plans were altered to include a second floor, which was then built to permit

the addition of a third floor above it. Then, a bedroom on the second floor of the mansion was converted into a Rare Books Room in 1986, complete with climate and temperature controls; the cost was largely borne by the Emma Elliott Women's Missionary Fellowship of the North Hills Reformed Presbyterian Church in suburban Pittsburgh. A renovation in 1999–2000 opened up a large area for books on biblical studies and created a Reformed Presbyterian Room; both are adjacent to the Rare Books Room. Another key part of the changes in 1999 was the installation of central air conditioning, providing a much better climate for the library—and its users!

The collections grew slowly from 4,000 volumes in 1900 to only 5,000 in 1950, a time period in which other seminaries were greatly augmenting their libraries, but then more energetically to 14,000 in 1973, 23,000 in 1983, 45,000 in 1996, and 65,000 today. In addition, several thousand items in other forms—microfiche and microfilm, audiovisuals, and online resources—have been added. The periodical collection has dramatically grown and improved, especially through aggressive use of the Periodical Exchange Program of the American Theological Library Association, beginning about 1982.

The acquisitions budget has been steadily increased, reaching $35,000 in 2008, which is supplemented by donations and gifts in kind made by many different people and organizations. Especially noteworthy were the collections given by the Willson family. Four successive generations of its members had taught at the seminary until that unlikely and unusual tradition came to an end. Another collection came from Pastor Ray Blair's widow, Clara, who had become the custodian of the library of the former Associate Presbyterian Church following Ray's sudden and early death. Both of these gifts were made in the early 1980s and took many years to process. When the library wing was added in 1970, the special speaker at the opening ceremony was Rev. Arthur Kuschke, who spent almost his entire working life building the outstanding Montgomery Library at Westminster Theological Seminary in Philadelphia, Pennsylvania. He later commented that, at that time, the collection consisted largely of Covenanter books and periodicals. The same cannot be said today, as the library has come to represent the breadth and depth of the Reformed theological tradition, and those other works necessary to support the seminary's mushrooming programs.

> *The library has come to represent the breadth and depth of the Reformed theological tradition, and those other works necessary to support the seminary's mushrooming programs.*

Efforts at cataloging the book collection were made by several volunteers, including Mrs. Louvenia Brown, wife of Pastor Claude C. Brown, of the Selma Reformed Presbyterian Church in Alabama. But it was only in the late 1960s that permanent, professional staff were added. Miss JoAnne Luther, a graduate of Geneva College with a master of library science degree from Syracuse University, became the first full-time, professional librarian in 1970. She served until a certain seminary student (J. Bruce Martin, '73) won her heart and took her off to rural Nebraska to be a Reformed Presbyterian pastor's wife. She served for such a

short period of time that Professor of Old Testament
Clark Copeland was heard to say that the seminary
should not hire a single woman of marriageable age
as librarian again! However, JoAnne Martin was
followed by another single young woman, Anne
Frohlich, a member of the Orthodox Presbyterian
Church. When she left for another position, she
was succeeded by Rachel George, a member of the
Allegheny Reformed Presbyterian Church, in 1978.
The great-niece of one of the more prominent pro-
fessors of the seminary, R.J. George, author of the three-volume set *The Covenanter
Pastor*, she took a more than fifty-percent pay cut to leave her very responsible
position as head reference librarian at the main Carnegie Library of Pittsburgh to
work at the seminary. When Miss George retired in 1996, the first male librarian,
Thomas Reid, an ordained Reformed Presbyterian minister who had previously
served in the libraries at Westminster Theological Seminary in Philadelphia and
Reformed Theological Seminary in Jackson, Mississippi, was appointed.

It was Rachel George who began the computerization of the library's catalog,
using the OCLC (then called the Ohio Computer Library Center) system; RPTS was
one of the first libraries outside Ohio that joined OCLC and one of the first seminaries. Not only were new acquisitions cataloged online, but also all the books acquired
before 1978 were recataloged—and relabeled as well, since the library migrated from
the Union Seminary Classification system to the Library of Congress Classification.
The book collection was essentially cataloged by 1986, making the seminary's library
one of the first libraries of any kind to accomplish that goal that had once seemed to

many librarians to be impossible. Yet it would take another seventeen years to complete the online cataloging of the rest of the library's collections.

The library staff grew apace, with part-time assistants providing crucial backup to the librarian, no longer serving as a full-time librarian. Several assistants went on to other positions within the seminary, including the current secretary, Carol Edgar, and development assistant, Kim Backensto. Particularly noteworthy is the fact that, since 1999, retiree John May of the Beverly Heights Presbyterian Church in Mount Lebanon, Pennsylvania, has volunteered his time four or five days each week in the library. Other volunteers of note are Bill and Betty Calderwood of Sterling, Kansas, members of the Presbyterian Church (USA), but long-time friends of the Sterling Reformed Presbyterian Church and grandparents of a baptized member of the Topeka Reformed Presbyterian Church. Visiting for up to four weeks at a time, they have helped to complete a number of special projects, including the barcoding of the collection and the implementation of a turn-key, online library system in 2000.

Currently serving in the regular, though part-time, staff are Amy Spear Troup, a professional librarian who is the oldest child of long-time RPTS professor Wayne Spear and his wife, Mary, and the wife of Adjunct Professor Calvin Troup of Duquesne University; Kristina O'Neill Brehm, daughter of President Jerry O'Neill and his wife, Ann; and Noah Bailey, an RPTS student. Also, one student usually is assigned six hours of work in the library each week as part of his scholarship. Still, with all the different staff members, the total workforce comes to only a little more than two full-time equivalents.

The RPTS library provides most of the information needs of the professors and students, but, for many years, has had a formal agreement with the Barbour Library of the nearby Pittsburgh Theological Seminary (of the mainline Presbyterian Church), permitting our patrons to freely use the other facility, one of the fifteen largest theological seminaries in North America with 280,000 cataloged volumes. Electronic media continue to be added at RPTS, but remain fairly limited in the field of theology and certainly expensive by any standard. As a result, the library has only a few, focused online resources, for many years now housed in the Computer Center, which adjoins the library part of the seminary's building.

Graduates of the seminary enjoy lifetime borrowing privileges, but few benefit from the perk, although the library's catalog is available through the seminary's Web site and the U.S. Postal Service offers a low "media mail" rate for returning materials. Some have called the seminary western Pennsylvania's "best kept secret." Perhaps its library, finally a source of strength for the seminary, is its own "best kept secret."

Jerry F. O'Neill

Twelve seminary graduates have reflected on the past—on their days in the seminary. Several authors have described still other aspects of seminary life. Dr. Spear and Rev. Tom Reid have introduced us to two vital elements of the seminary—the faculty and the library. The book closes, fittingly, with a look to the future by Dr. Jerry O'Neill. After working in the administration of both Geneva and Sterling Colleges, Jerry entered the seminary in 1979. In 1981 he became pastor in Columbus, Indiana, until elected by Synod in 1994 to be the seminary's president. President O'Neill and his wife, Ann, are parents of five children.

CHAPTER 17

Looking to the Future

In a unique and wonderful way, I have had the privilege of serving the Lord and the Reformed Presbyterian Church of North America for the past several years as president of the Reformed Presbyterian Theological Seminary. Never could I have anticipated the joy and sense of fulfillment that would be mine by serving the Lord in this capacity! Truly, the Lord is at work among us, and I can happily testify to His abundant goodness and mercy.

When I came to this seminary as a student in 1979 at the age of 32, I was reluctant to move my wife and children from central Kansas to a city in Pennsylvania that my dad once described in jest as best seen in a rearview mirror! I thought that there must surely be a way to do long-distance theological education in a manner that would prepare me sufficiently for pastoral ministry without such a move. I was an ordained deacon in my local congregation at the time, was working in a very satisfying job at Sterling College, and the thought of moving was not an altogether pleasant one.

But when I began my studies at RPTS, I soon realized that there was much to learn at the seminary that I simply would not have gotten elsewhere. It was, in many ways, a life-changing experience for me. Most importantly I learned that I did not know nearly as much as I thought I did. I also became convicted of certain foundational truths of Scripture that previously had only been a mystery to me. I greatly appreciate my years of training at RPTS, and I believe that this training has been foundational to everything else that I have done since then.

In particular, as I reflect on my student days at the seminary, I remember the teaching of Dr. Wayne Spear, Dr. Clark Copeland, Dr. Renwick Wright, and Dr. Bruce Stewart. These men were excellent in every way. Dr. Spear was clear, methodical and systematic; Dr. Copeland was challenging and full of new insights—new to me—for understanding the Scriptures; Dr. Wright was a godly scholar-pastor and a friend; and Dr. Stewart was kind, encouraging, diligent and able to teach. Of course, the out-of-class discussions with fellow students, including Jonathan Watt, Marty Wilsey and Bob Schmidtberger, were enlightening and stimulating as well.

I greatly appreciate my years of training at RPTS, and I believe that this training has been foundational to everything alse that I have done since then.

In the kind providence of God, I returned to the Reformed Presbyterian Theological Seminary in 1995 to serve as president and as professor of Pastoral Theology. In these intervening years, I have often reflected on a comment made a number of years ago by the late Professor John Gerstner when he addressed the RPCNA Synod, emphasizing the fact that no other seminary has existed in our country for even 150 years without turning toward theological liberalism and relativism. What a sobering thought!

As I have reflected on the difference between our seminary and most of the other seminaries that have not remained true to their founding principles, it has become more and more clear to me that the close oversight of the seminary by the Synod of the Reformed Presbyterian Church of North America has been the instrument used by God to keep the seminary faithful to the historic Christian

faith. To the extent that the denomination remains faithful and continues direct oversight of its seminary, this institution should remain doctrinally sound. And to the extent that the seminary remains true to the historic faith as articulated and defended by our demonination, there should be faithful pastors trained at the seminary who will, in turn, serve the next generation of the denomination without doctrinal compromise. In this way, the cycle continues; and in this way, if God is so pleased to bless and prosper, the historic faith should be passed down from one generation to the next until our Lord Jesus Christ returns.

When I think of the future of RPTS, my one great desire is for the seminary to remain faithful to the Lord, to His Word, and to the mission He has given us. If we are faithful, the Lord will bless. If we are not faithful, then I would not want to see the seminary continue, even if in the eyes of the world we were to prosper.

Our fundamental mission at RPTS has always been to train pastors for the sponsoring denomination, but the Lord has clearly expanded our mission in the last half-century to train pastors and other church leaders from a variety of denominational and cultural backgrounds for various missions and ministries of the church. This is as exciting as it is challenging!

As I write this article, it is the goal of the board and administration to see more students from other Reformed denominations study at RPTS, and we are eager for our current ministry to Pittsburgh's urban community to continue

to prosper. Our close working relationship with the Center for Urban Biblical Ministry has been a tremendous blessing for the seminary, and we trust that we are being used by the Lord to bless the churches in Pittsburgh as well. We also hope to foster our relationship with international students, who seem to thrive in the intimate family atmosphere at RPTS.

Even as this article is written, we are beginning a doctor of ministry program that we believe will supplement our MDiv and MTS programs. Our goal in the DMin program is to encourage and strengthen pastors who sense a need for further training. There is also a desire on the part of some to offer a master of theology (ThM) degree in future years. Another future development may well be the use of the Internet to provide certain courses online. This could potentially improve our service to the Reformed Presbyterian Church and also increase our opportunities to meet needs of the Church throughout the world.

As we look to our third century of service to Christ, we are admittedly in a time of transition. Men who have served faithfully at RPTS for many long years are no longer in full-time service. Younger men are taking up the responsibilities passed down to them. No longer are we a Scotch-Irish institution. Professors and adjunct professors include such names as Backensto, Selvaggio and Prutow—quite different from having the Scotch-Irish ring of Stewart, Wright and Copeland. This is a good thing, and we rejoice in God's good provision in expanding the ministry of the RPCNA far beyond our cultural heritage.

We are committed to building three qualities into the lives of our students as we look to the future. First, we want our graduates to be spiritually mature, loving Christ and one another, filled with the fruit of righteousness that comes through Jesus Christ. Second, we want our graduates to be knowledgeable and committed to the Reformed faith, with an eagerness to be lifelong learners. Third, we want our graduates to be able to teach others all that God has taught them, able to teach and preach and counsel with skill and compassion.

Of course none of this is new. That is exactly what our forefathers strove to teach those whom they trained. Thus, as we look to the future, we realize in a sense that we have come full-circle, and that we are called to do in the next century exactly what those who have gone before us have done: to train gifted, godly and theologically knowledgeable and committed students who will devote their lives to service in Christ's Kingdom. If our sovereign God enables us to do this with excellence and faithfulness and for His glory, we can have every confidence that our labors will not be in vain; and that He will bless our labors in His timing, and for His purposes, as the Lord Jesus Christ continues to build His Church and extend His Kingdom.

...and for His glory

They go from strength to strength

PSALM 84:7*a*

APPENDIX:
PICTORIAL INDEX

(Identifications are from left to right)